MARK: GOOD NEWS FOR HARD TIMES

The scripture quotations used in this book are from the
Revised Standard Version of the Bible, copyrighted 1946,
1952 © 1971, 1973 by the Division of Christian Education of
the National Council of the Churches of Christ in the
U.S.A., and used by permission.

Published by Franciscan University Press
Franciscan University of Steubenville
Steubenville, Ohio 43952

Cover Design by Daniel Gallio

Published in the United States of America

ISBN 0-940535-53-X

MARK
Good News for Hard Times

A Popular Commentary on the Earliest Gospel

George T. Montague, S.M.

FRANCISCAN UNIVERSITY PRESS
Steubenville, Ohio 43952

Contents

Chapter	Title	Scripture Verses	Page
1.	John Heralds the Mightier One	1:1-8	11
2.	Jesus Is Baptized	1:9-11	14
3.	Jesus in the Desert	1:12-13	16
4.	Jesus Begins His Ministry	1:14-15	18
5.	Fishers of Men	1:16-20	21
6.	A New Teaching with Authority	1:21-28	23
7.	A Healing Service—What to Do with Success	1:29-39	26
8.	Jesus Cures a Leper	1:40-45	28
9.	Jesus and the Paralytic	2:1-12	31
10.	Jesus, The Caller and Teacher of Sinners	2:13-17	34
11.	On Feasting and Fasting	2:18-22	37
12.	Lord of the Sabbath	2:23-28	39
13.	To Save Life or To Kill?	3:1-6	42
14.	Brighter Light, Darker Shadows	3:7-19	44
15.	The Spirit in Jesus — Jesus' New Family	3:19-35	47
16.	Sower, Seed, and Soil	4:1-20	51
17.	The Lamp and the Measure	4:21-25	55
18.	The Mystery of Growth	4:26-34	57
19.	Lord of Wind and Sea	4:35-41	60
20.	Jesus Frees and Restores	5:1-20	62
21.	Jesus Conquers Even Death	5:21-43	66
22.	Rejection at Home	6:1-6	70
23.	Jesus Sends the Twelve	6:6-13	73
24.	A Slain Prophet Lives On	6:14-29	75
25.	Bread in the Wilderness	6:30-44	79
26.	Encounter at Sea	6:45-52	82
27.	Jesus Liberates God's Word	6:53-7:23	84
28.	Healer Without Frontiers	7:24-30	88
29.	"He Has Done All Things Well"	7:31-37	91
30.	Look Beyond the Bread	8:1-21	93

Preface to the Second Printing

Eleven years have passed since *Mark: Good News for Hard Times* was first published. Since the book went out of print I have received requests from many quarters, especially from teachers and leaders of Bible studies, to reprint the work. Other than a few minor corrections, no changes have been made in the present text. The enduring value of the original work makes the expense of major revisions unwarranted. I would like, however, to make a few comments here about the more important developments in Markan studies in the last few years.

Most significant have been the studies of Mark as a literary and narrative work. The results have confirmed more than ever that Mark is not a haphazard collection of stories about Jesus and some of His sayings. Instead, his gospel is a carefully crafted masterpiece in which traditional materials have been melded together in a way that leads the reader rapidly and inexorably to the climax of the cross and the empty tomb.

I would especially recommend an easy-to-read book by David Rhoads and Donald Miche, *Mark as Story: An Introduction to the Narrative of a Gospel* (Philadelphia: Fortress Press, 1982), which studies Mark's narrative patterns, his development of settings, characters and plot. None of their conclusions contradict those of this book but rather enhances them.

What interests me and most readers is Mark's message—or, if you will, his theology: in his reporting and interpreting of the tradition about Jesus, what is he trying to tell us?

George T. Montague, S.M.
August 14, 1992

Preface

Bread For You

This book began when I was asked by the editor of *New Covenant* to do a monthly "Scripture Companion" for the magazine. I welcomed the opportunity to address a wide audience of Christians who had a hunger for the bread of God's word available to them in the scriptures. In that audience there were some, I was certain, who were Bible readers of long standing but who had little appreciation of the positive contributions of historical biblical scholarship. There were others, including many Roman Catholics, for whom the Bible was still a great unknown, and who were only exposed to it in ocassional liturgical readings. There were others who were confused by statements of biblical scholars which challenged their treasured beliefs about the scriptures. Finally, there were a vast number of readers who had just come into a personal relationship with the Lord and were experiencing the power of the Holy Spirit in a new way. These were looking in the scriptures for guidance and nourishment for prayer.

Was it possible to meet all these needs in a single, simple scripture commentary? It was something of a challenge to my scholarship, but even more a challenge to my ability to listen to the scriptures in a prayerful way, respecting God's truth on all sides. That meant truly *under-standing* the scriptures—standing under them as God's word, but also standing under them as his word made flesh in a given segment of human history, culture, language, and mediated through a human author and all the processes such an author goes through to write a book. Then, the conviction that these words not only meant something when they were written but also mean something today confronted me with the further challenge: What is God saying to me, to us, to the world today in these words written nearly two millenia ago? And finally, could I communicate all this in such a way that my readers could respond, "Amen"?

1

I might have given up had not my first attempts at the monthly feature been greeted with an enthusiastic response by the readers of *New Covenant*. There was only one problem: At the rate I was going, to cover the Gospel of Mark in a monthly feature would take over five years! After two years of monthly installments, I decided to complete the commentary and prepare it for publication as a book. The editor of *New Covenant* and I decided that, in order to reach the end of Mark quickly, the monthly installments in the magazine would be expanded, and only highlights of the remaining commentary would be used. For the book, we decided that I would revise and expand the commentary itself and that the Revised Standard Version of Mark would be supplied in the text for easy reference. Aids to study, sharing, and prayer would also be provided to make this commentary as versatile as possible for a variety of uses.

I have added a final chapter after the commentary, summing up what I consider Mark's most important insights for Christian discipleship today.

God's word is bread made of the finest wheat (Ps 147:14; Dt 8:3). But the making of bread is a long process. The wheat must be harvested from the fields, crushed into flour, mixed with leaven, condiments, and liquid. Then it is allowed to rise, kneaded or beaten to distribute the leaven evenly, and properly baked. In this book I have harvested the wheat of God's word from Mark's field, crushed it through study of the situation in which it was written and the situation in which it is read today, mixed in the leaven of the Spirit and prayer, and tested these insights by the Christian tradition—thus, hopefully, beating down any knowledge that merely puffs up rather than builds (1 Cor 8:1). If I may add a modern touch to this already complex image, I have frozen this readied dough in the words of this book.

But there is one more step. You, the reader, must do the baking. Take these words out of the deep-freeze, put them in the spirit-warmed oven of your heart, and let them become the bread of God's word for you.

Introduction

I

The Bible is the word of God.

That means many things, but most importantly it means that the word is a *personal* word. It comes from a person and is a way in which that person makes himself present to another. When we analyze God's word under the microscope of historical or literary science, we can all too easily forget that there is a Person behind that word. When a doctor uses sophisticated instruments to examine a patient, he may be looking at one particular organ, but he should never forget that this is also *someone* he is treating.

So likewise with God's word. There is of course an objective and measurable element about it, but it never ceases to be the word of a person. It never ceases to be the word *of God*. This is what we believe as Christians.

Let's call this aspect of the word its subjectivity—that is, its rootedness in the person whose expression and communication it is. Now when God speaks his word to the world, he does not leave it floating in an "objective" state. It is not unattached, un-subjectivized, un-personed, and un-shepherded, in a way that would make it available to people who want to approach it in a "detached" way—detached from their own personal involvement and detached from the God who speaks it. Of course, since God chooses human words and human instruments to convey his words, it is possible for the hearers to simply latch on to the humanly objectivized words, dispute their meaning, interpret them as they wish, and thus become, in effect, the "sole proprietors" of the words. Jesus' words were misunderstood by many, even by his own disciples at times, and he had to assure them that "the flesh" is useless to understand his words; only the Spirit can give life and understanding (Jn 6:63).

3

The Personal Word Is Entrusted . . .

If we look at how God revealed himself in the Old and the New Testaments, we see that he entrusted his subjectivity to the subjectivity of chosen persons, so that *his* word became *their* word. And it was no less *their* word for its being *God's*, and no less *God's* word for being *theirs*. After all, when the Lord revealed himself to Moses in the burning bush, he said, "I am the God of your father, the God of Abraham, the God of Isaac, the God of Jacob" (Ex 3:6). He is the God whom no man can see and live (Ex 33:20); he can be known in this life only indirectly, through his word as received and experienced in the lives of his chosen ones. This movement reaches its high point in Jesus Christ, of whom John says, "No one has ever seen God. The only Son, who is God, ever at the Father's side, has revealed him" (Jn 1:18). The effect of Jesus' coming, his preaching, his life, his ministry, his death and glorification, is that the Father whom he calls "my God" now becomes for the disciples "your God" (Jn 20:17).

. . . To Jesus and to the Church

In Jesus the mystery of the interpersonalness of the word reaches its summit: "My word," he says, "is not my own" (Jn 14:24). St. Augustine ponders this paradox. If it is "my word," he says, how can it *not* be "my word"? And if it is someone else's word, how can it be mine? The heart of the mystery is that God confides his word to Jesus, and Jesus is so at one with the Father that the Father's word is also his. Though it is mind-boggling, we can understand how God might have done this for Jesus, who, after all, was God's own word in person, his Son. But how could God have done it for anyone else? How could he have risked to confide his word to the disciples, to the church? And yet that is exactly what we read in the New Testament: "He who hears you hears me" (Lk 10:16); "he who receives you receives me, and he who receives me receives him who sent me" (Mt 10:40).

The word of God never gets lost in the void. It is always

someone's word. This is particularly true of the gospels. They are intended to be, first of all, a report about God's plan of salvation in Jesus Christ, or "what Jesus did and taught" (Acts 1:1). That is, at their deepest level they are meant to communicate Jesus' view of things, his message, his life, his mighty deeds. But none of the evangelists was standing by taking down in shorthand what Jesus said. We know that Luke was not himself an eyewitness of Jesus' ministry, and the same is probably true of Mark. After the events of Jesus' life, death, and resurrection, there was a long intervening period in which the tradition about Jesus circulated orally, relived by those inside the various Christian communities and preached to those outside. The word of Jesus had become the word of Peter and Andrew, James and John, and subsequently the word of the communities that grew to maturity by pondering and reliving those events and teachings, finding meaning for their lives in them. We can speak of the emergence of a Christian memory, a memory which the Spirit of prophecy, active in the new communities, respected and built upon. The Coming One, for whose return the Spirit of prophecy inspired an ever-greater longing (Rv 22:17), was also the one who had come.

Now this memory bank, kept alive and freshly applied to new situations in the Christian communities, became the source of the oral tradition about Jesus. Christians spoke of it as the word of Jesus and even the word of God, but it was also the word of the Jerusalem community, of the Antioch community, of the Roman community, and so on. And out of the large fund of Jesus' words and traditions about him, those which lasted were those which responded to specific practical needs of the community: preaching outlines, guides for daily living, answers to questions in debates with non-Christians, a canon for the celebration of the Lord's supper, and so on. Underlying all these needs was the desire to build up the faith (Jn 20:31), but each community also had its own particular concerns. The concerns in Rome were not always the same as the concerns in Jerusalem or Antioch or Ephesus. This explains why the traditions about Jesus developed in different ways in different communities, just as today we find different Christian communities developing a certain spirituality of their own within the broad spectrum of possibilities opened by the word of God.

This also explains why the traditions about Jesus were modified in the process so as to make a clear application to a new culture and a new situation. The words of the Lord's prayer, for example, are not exactly the same in Luke as in Matthew. Matthew's version represents a more typically Jewish formulation in places while Luke's is shorter. Which is more original? At first sight we might think the more Jewish is the more original. But in this case it is just as likely that the Jewish community (or Matthew) "fleshed out" the bare outline of the prayer with well-known phrases from the rich Jewish liturgical tradition. In any case, we have to acknowledge that in this early period there were two complementary tendencies: (1) a tendency to keep and repeat the words and deeds of Jesus just as they were handed down (Lk 1:2); and (2) a sovereign, Spirit-led freedom to incarnate the living message in ways demanded by changing culture, language, and circumstance.

Jesus' word thus became the church's word. And eventually, the word became the evangelist's word.

II

The Evangelist's Word

During the period when the tradition about Jesus was being handed on, applied, and enriched orally, some of the sayings of Jesus were written down. One of these collections seems to have been available to both Luke and Matthew, since they both have many sayings of Jesus which Mark does not have. This collection, sometimes called "Q" (from the German *Quelle* or "Source"), had little narrative. It probably served as an early catechism of the teaching of Jesus, but it was not yet a gospel.

Quite early, however, one important piece of narrative material was written down—the story of Jesus' passion and death. We know this must have been done early because the accounts in Mark, Matthew, and Luke are so close in their agreement that the tradition seems to have been frozen at an early stage. This is understandable considering the primary interest the early disciples must have had in recounting those most precious hours of their Master's life—his final encounter with the malice of men which fulfilled, in an unexpected way, the prophecy of the Suffering Servant. Not only was this story cherished within the communities. It was also important to show both Jew and Gentile how the paradox happened—that he who preached the kingdom of God, healing and delivering, should end up rejected and crucified. This also explains in part why Christians eventually wanted an "orderly account" from the beginning (Lk 1:3). They had lived for years listening to fragments of the oral tradition, or to skeletal outlines of preaching, like Peter's in Acts (1:21-22; 2:22-36; 3:12-26; 10:34-43). Now they needed a historian in the real sense of the term—that is, not a collector of facts and texts but one who could put them all together in a meaningful way. This process was already begun in the oral preaching, of course. But the time came when it should be committed to writing.

The writers, called evangelists, brought the process of interpretative reporting to a new level. Each had a message for his particular community, a teaching which at times simply put the community's traditions into writing and at other times brought new and needed emphases to the life of the community.

In short we can say that each evangelist: (1) was himself formed by the tradition in which he lived and the community to which he belonged; (2) was a reporter and transmitter of that tradition, in the sense that he felt obliged to hand it on with as much integrity as possible (we will note in Mark especially how he often does this at the expense of literary smoothness); (3) was also a creative interpreter of that tradition, standing above the community for which he wrote as an inspired preacher might consider himself standing above the community when preaching God's word to it.

This is the sense in which we understand each evangelist to be inspired. He was not inspired to create out of thin air. Much of his material lay before him in oral and some in written form.

The inspiration of the Holy Spirit bore upon the creative way he would select, organize, and shape these materials so that the old message would also be new and living—it would be the *evangelist's* own message to the church. In studying each of the gospels, it is important to understand the mind of the evangelist, for ultimately it is always through his eyes that we are seeing Jesus and the church. Each evangelist is more than a reporter. He is a composer, an artist, a theologian, interpreting as he reports.

III

The Gospel of Mark

The gospel according to Mark could be called a "Handbook for Hard Times." The majority of scholars agree it was written in the late sixties in Rome as an encouragement to Christians suffering persecution under Nero. Tacitus, the Roman historian writing a generation after the events, says that Nero found in the Christians a scapegoat for the widespread fire that Suetonius says Nero himself started. Christians were rounded up, some of them crucified, some torn apart by wild beasts, some made into human torches. Large numbers were faithful even in the face of death, but some broke under torture and betrayed their fellow Christians. It was a crisis the likes of which the Roman Christians had never seen, but those first generation missionaries who had come from Palestine could recall the dark hours of Jesus' own passion and death. There is a strong tradition that one of them, Simon Peter, had come to Rome and there shared his own memories of Jesus' life and death. There Peter had ample occasion to atone for his own weakness, for, according to tradition, he died a martyr's death in the same chaotic storm that swept scores of Christians to the arena or to the gardens of Nero.

It was after Peter's death that Mark set to work to write a gospel—the first complete work of its kind—as an encouragement to the embattled Christians of Rome. This Mark is no doubt the same John Mark who accompanied Paul and Barnabas on part of their first missionary journey (Acts 12:25; 13:13) and who later came to Rome and worked with Paul (Phlm 24; Col 4:10) and with Peter (1 Pt 5:13). Papias, around 140 A.D., tells us that Mark was the interpreter of Peter, that he wrote down whatever Peter remembered of the things said and done by the Lord, though not in order. This does not mean that Mark was merely a recorder of Peter's preaching. Historical evidence points to the fact that Mark wrote after Peter's death, and while much of the tradition as Mark remembered it had a Petrine stamp, some of it no doubt came from other sources, some of which may have already been in written form.

Whatever the materials Mark had to work with, it is clear that he was a composer in a true sense. His gospel reflects here and there the crisis situation in which the Roman Christians found themselves. "Every one will be salted with fire" (Mk 9:49). This curious, detached saying of Jesus, found only in Mark, is hard to understand by itself and even in the context in which it appears with other sayings. But as a description of Christian martyrdom, it would be particularly meaningful in the kind of persecution Tacitus describes.

Jesus was driven into the desert where he was with the wild beasts (1:13); Christians facing the beasts of the arena could well remember their Master! Jesus promised his followers a hundred-fold in this life—along with persecutions (10:30). He promised persecution and betrayal even by one's family (13:1-13). And his own life ended with death upon the cross, a fate he said every disciple must be willing to share (8:34-35). What won the faith of the Roman centurion (a Markan representation of the well-disposed pagans of Rome?) was not a miraculous last-minute delivery of Jesus from the cross. It was not even the resurrection. Rather, it was the heroic way in which Jesus died (15:39). So too, Mark is saying, Christians must not expect to be spared a martyr's death. If they expect to win the faith of the Roman world, it will be by their heroism, even to the cross. Thus, discipleship in Mark is by definition heroic—a discipleship of the cross. For Jesus himself reveals who he is—the Messiah and the Son of God—precisely in the power and the pain of the cross (1:1; 8:29-38; 15:39).

John Heralds the Mightier One

1:1-8

1 The beginning of the gospel of Jesus Christ, the Son of God. ²As it is written in Isaiah the prophet,

"Behold, I send my messenger before thy face,
who shall prepare thy way;
³the voice of one crying in the wilderness:
Prepare the way of the Lord,
make his paths straight—"

⁴John the baptizer appeared in the wilderness, preaching a baptism of repentance for the forgiveness of sins. ⁵And there went out to him all the country of Judea, and all the people of Jerusalem; and they were baptized by him in the river Jordan, confessing their sins. ⁶Now John was clothed with camel's hair, and had a leather girdle around his waist, and ate locusts and wild honey. ⁷And he preached, saying, "After me comes he who is mightier than I, the thong of whose sandals I am not worthy to stoop down and untie. ⁸I have baptized you with water; but he will baptize you with the Holy Spirit."

WHEN PETER EXPLAINED to the community gathered in the upper room why Judas' place among the Twelve had to be filled, he said that to be a candidate for this position a man had to have been a witness from the beginning—and "the beginning" meant the baptism of John (Acts 1:22). That is why Mark's gospel, following the same pattern, tells us that this is where the good news really began. Certainly it had been in preparation and promise a long time, as the prophecies quoted bear out. But here, on the Jordan river bank, it broke into the public forum as fulfillment.

Notice the titles Mark gives Jesus in the opening line: He is Messiah (Christ) and Son of God. The gospel is built around the gradual revelation on the part of God and Jesus of these two aspects of Jesus' identity. It is a gradual discovery by the disciples and the Gentiles, and most of all, by the Christians who follow the unfolding of Mark's account. The first part of the gospel builds up to Peter's confession that Jesus is the Messiah (8:29); the climax of the second part is the centurion's confession that Jesus is the Son of God (15:39).

The Old Testament passage cited here is actually a fusion of three scripture texts, of which only the last (vs. 3) is from Isaiah (40:3). Such fusion of texts was common practice among the rabbis, who even prior to Mark had combined the texts from Exodus 23:20 and Malachi 3:1 to show that the "messenger of the covenant" is Elijah (Mal 4:5; 3:23). More importantly for Mark, the text from Exodus evokes the divine messenger ("angel" in some translations—the meaning is the same) who was sent to lead the Israelites of the first Exodus through the desert to the promised land. The second Exodus, the return from the captivity of Babylon, was also a journey through the desert, and the road was likewise prepared by a messenger, a herald (Is 40:3). Now these scriptures have come to fulfillment in the person and mission of John the Baptist, who tells the people to "prepare the way of the Lord." The Greek text of the last line of Isaiah 40:3 had read "the paths of God," but Mark alters it to read *"his* paths," so that it can be applied to the "Lord" who has just been mentioned—no longer the Yahweh of the Old Testament but Jesus, the Lord of the New.

The desert had not only been the place of the Lord's original covenant with his people, nor was it merely the passageway for a return to the holy land. From the time of Hosea onward, it was held to be the place where the Lord would renew his people in righteousness, love, mercy, and fidelity (Hos 2:21-22), where he would once again speak to the heart of his bride and espouse her to him forever, so that she would truly "know the Lord" (Hos 2:16-25). Even in Old Testament times, renewal movements like the Rekabites (Jer 35) felt that only in the desert could the God of Sinai be met and served with purity. So too it would be with Qumran, the monastery by the Dead Sea.

John's appearance in the desert would have evoked these memories. He exists on desert fare and wears the garment Elijah wore (2 Kgs 1:8). This detail is a forecast of 9:9-13 where John will be explicitly identified with the prophet.

John's preaching evoked a response that was ritualized in a baptism expressive of repentance. Jewish tradition knew of ritual washings, and such washings were especially important at Qumran, the monastery, probably Essene, situated not far from where John was baptizing. But John's rite means a complete return to God, heart and soul, in the hope of receiving the total forgiveness of sins. Why is this imperative and urgent? Not, in Mark's view, because "the kingdom of God is at hand" (as in Mt 3:2) but because "after me comes he who is mightier than I" (1:7). "The mightier one" is not a messianic title; it is a mysterious name setting the stage for the binding of the strong man (Jesus is the mightier one, 3:27) and, in the immediate context, for the superior power of baptism with the Holy Spirit. In Hebrew or Aramaic this latter term can mean a "spirit of holiness." What John probably meant by it was that the Spirit with which "the Stronger One" would baptize would be a purifying fire of holiness before which only the repentant could survive (cf. Is 4:4).

Jesus Is Baptized

1:9-11

⁹In those days Jesus came from Nazareth of Galilee and was baptized by John in the Jordan. ¹⁰And when he came up out of the water, immediately he saw the heavens opened and the Spirit descending upon him like a dove; ¹¹and a voice from heaven, "Thou art my beloved Son; with thee I am well pleased."

AFTER THE TRUMPET-LIKE announcement of the Coming One, the mightier Baptizer with the Holy Spirit, verse 9 cannot but appear as anti-climactic, but Mark intends it to be so, revealing in the first mention of Jesus' name the "secret" nature of his coming. In contrast to the multitudes, the Baptizer with the Holy Spirit comes alone. He comes from Galilee and not, as did the others, from Jerusalem—the center of orthodox Judaism. And he comes first to receive rather than to give. By queuing up with the penitents and letting himself be immersed by John in the waters, he identifies totally with repentant Israel. Thus, before calling Israel to repentance, he first identifies with Israel, with her sinfulness and her need for cleansing. As Jesus will emerge from the waters in which the people are baptized, so will he emerge from their midst as the Messiah. He is not, at least for now, an overpowering heavenly deliverer, but rather the humble servant whose life is given for the ransom of the multitude (cf. 10:45).

But already now, to Jesus and to the Christian reader of Mark, the true identity of Jesus is revealed. To his *coming up* out of the waters there is a corresponding *coming down* on the part of God, as the rending of the heavens in Isaiah 64:1 suggests: "Oh, that thou wouldst rend the heavens and come down. . . ." As the Lord of the first Exodus came down only after the people had been consecrated (Ex 19:10-11), so the rending of the heavens, the appearance of the Spirit, and the heavenly voice now mean a new relationship made possible by the consecration of Jesus in the Jordan.

In Is 63:10-11, the poet, yearning for a new deliverance by the Lord, recalls how the Lord led up from the waters of the sea the great shepherd Moses and put his holy spirit in the midst of his people. The themes of spirit, water, and desert were frequent descriptions of the coming age of salvation (Is 32:15; 44:3). Mark sees all this fulfilled in a supreme way in the theophany as Jesus comes up from the water. The image of the dove suggests, however, that there is more than a new Exodus happening here. A first-century rabbinic tradition explained the Spirit hovering over the waters at the creation in Genesis 1:2 with the image of a dove. Mark then may be suggesting more than the fact that Jesus is the true Israel (frequently personified in Jewish tradition as a dove). He means that with Jesus the Spirit hovering over the baptismal waters has begun a new creation of the world.

"Thou art my beloved Son; with thee I am well pleased" is not an exact quotation from the Old Testament, but it does echo the messianic Psalm 2:7, "You are my Son"; and the Servant Song of Isaiah 42:1, "Behold my servant, whom I have chosen, in whom my soul delights; I have put my Spirit upon him." Jesus is thus Messiah and Spirit-bearing Servant, but most of all he is *Son*. As W.L. Lane and others have pointed out, "Thou *art*" suggests an eternal relationship. Since the Greek aorist translated by the Revised Standard Version as "with thee I am well pleased" really means a past choice for a particular mission. The combined meaning, then, is: "Because you are my unique Son, I have chosen you for the task upon which you are about to enter."

Mark gives us no indication of anyone seeing or hearing the theophany other than Jesus himself (and the Christian reader, of course). For the moment, Jesus is still the hidden Messiah-Servant-Son who comes as a penitent. Only through his Spirit-led action will the outer world begin to learn who he is.

Jesus in the Desert

1:12-13

¹²The Spirit immediately drove him out into the wilderness. ¹³And he was in the wilderness forty days, tempted by Satan; and he was with the wild beasts; and the angels ministered to him.

VERSES 12 AND 13 conclude what might be called Mark's prologue. Hardly has Jesus been baptized, with the manifestation of the Spirit and the designation by the heavenly voice, than he is *driven* (Matthew and Luke use a milder term) into the desert by the Spirit. The word *Spirit* occurs three times in this prologue and binds together the promise by the Baptist (v. 8), the baptism of Jesus (v. 10), and the desert temptation (v. 12). Clearly for Jesus, the possession of the Spirit and his designation as God's son are not meant to spare him struggle and conflict. As Jesus shared the lot of repentant Israel by entering the waters of baptism, so he now shares the lot of ancient Israel by entering the place where Israel was tempted and failed—the desert.

Israel wandered there for forty years. Moses stayed on Mount Sinai forty days and forty nights (Ex 24:18), and Elijah spent forty days journeying there (1 Kgs 19:8). The number forty is symbolic, therefore, of an important period of testing, preparation, or encounter. Here it is primarily testing.

Mark is not concerned, as are Matthew and Luke, with the specific temptations but with the fact that the entire period is one of conflict, and the adversary is Satan. By introducing this protagonist, Mark informs us from the very beginning that Jesus' ministry will be a wrestling not with flesh and blood but with principalities and powers (cf. Eph 6:12). Jesus' conflict with Satan does not end in the desert: it only begins there. In his public ministry he will confront Satan in those possessed (1:23; 5:2; 7:25; 9:17, etc.), in the testing questions of his opponents (8:11; 10:2; 12:15; cf. 8:33), and even in the blind resistance of his own disciples (8:33). Satan is the strong man, but Jesus has come as the stronger one to bind him (1:7; 3:27). If we would understand Jesus as Mark understands him, we must accept this role of demonic antagonism throughout the gospel.

Why does Mark mention the wild beasts? In Psalm 91, protection by the angels and conquest over the wild beasts is promised to him who clings to the Lord in time of temptation. Was Mark thinking of this passage, as Luke and Matthew obviously were (Lk 4:10; Mt 4:6)? Or was he thinking of those passages of the Old Testament where the desert is transformed into a paradise with no wild beasts in it (Is 35:9; Ez 34:23-28)? Or was he thinking of the age of perfection when the wild animals will no longer harm anyone (Is 11:6-9; cf. Is 43:19-20)? The problem here is that Jesus is not described as struggling with the beasts or conquering them, nor is it said that he pacified them. He was *with* them. Is this restraint in Mark calculated to prepare the reader for the further conflict to ensue in the rest of the gospel? Is it a reminder to the Christians of Rome that they may, like their Master, have to meet the wild beasts in the sands of the arena? Since the text does not compel any one of these meanings to the exclusion of the others, the reader may choose the interpretation he or she prefers.

Angels ministered to Jesus. In the first Exodus in the desert, an angel, later identified as the Lord's "holy spirit" (Is 63:9-10), had an important function in leading the people (Ex 14:19; 23:20, 23; 32:34; 33:2). An angel ministered in the desert to Elijah, bringing him food and drink (1 Kgs 19:5-7). Although Mark is too brief in his allusions to satisfy our desire for clarity, what is important for Christians to know is that if God calls them into the desert, he will nourish them there (cf. Rev 12:6) as he did Jesus.

Thus the stage is set for the cosmic struggle to be witnessed by men. In this opening prologue Mark has been speaking to the church in Rome, reminding it that the gift of the Spirit and the divine sonship it enjoys are no guarantee against struggle and persecution. On the contrary, the first effect of the Spirit is to lead to the desert—a place of divine encounter, yes, but also the place for the struggle with Satan. However fearsome the desert may be, and even if they have to struggle with wild beasts in it (cf. 1 Cor 15:32), God will care for his people there. For so it was with Jesus, whose whole ministry the reader is now prepared to understand.

4

Jesus Begins His Ministry
1:14-15

¹⁴Now after John was arrested, Jesus came into Galilee, preaching the gospel of God, ¹⁵and saying, "The time is fulfilled, and the kingdom of God is at hand; repent, and believe in the gospel."

MARK CONSIDERS JESUS' relation to John the Baptist an important one. John heralded Jesus, but Jesus begins his ministry only after John has been violently swept off the scene. "Delivered up" means arrested and imprisoned. The same word will be later used as a technical term for Jesus' own being "delivered up" to the political authorities (9:31; 14:10; 15:1) and to scourging and crucifixion (15:15). Mark is hinting already in the gospel that Jesus will be one with John not only in calling for repentance but in suffering martyrdom.

Only later will we be told the details of John's martyrdom (6:14-29). At this point they would distract from the figure of Jesus who now solemnly begins his ministry. Though heralded by John, Jesus is himself herald. A herald does not teach or reason or entertain or negotiate. He announces. To "preach" means in the first place to *proclaim* something. In Jesus' case it is "God's good news." In Greek, *euangelion* means the kind of good news announced at the birth of a new king or, more often, the good news of victory in war. For the Jew, from Isaiah onward (40:9), it meant the moment of the Lord's promised deliverance of his people—from their slavery in Babylon or from whatever oppression they were experiencing.

This moment of expected deliverance was called the "kingdom of God." Why was this term used, and what did it mean? "Kingdom" is often understood as a place, like the miniature kingdom of Monaco. In the gospels, however, it means not realm but rule—God's entering upon his rule in time and history, the moment when he will enforce justice and vindicate his people.

From the time of the Sinai covenant, the people of Israel had learned to think of the Lord as king. They were his covenanted vassals, and he their vindicator, their champion. When oppressed by enemies or victimized by their foe's power, the Lord's people could stand on this covenant relationship and cry to him, not just as to a sovereign power but as to their own king, to whom they belonged. Later a complacency about this relationship developed, so God sent the prophets to remind the people that his rule is also a purifying judgment for sinners. Even so, Israel never lost sight of the Lord as her king. In fact, the longing for him to exercise his kingship became only more acute. By Jesus' time, Israel had spent centuries under the dominion of the Babylonian kings, the Persians, the Greeks, and finally the Roman emperors.

What would happen when God began this reign so ardently hoped for? One would see on a divine scale what happened only ritually and in hope whenever Israel's kings of old would take the throne (see Pss 2, 110), or when the Lord's own enthronement was celebrated in the temple (see Pss 47, 96, 97, 99): The scepter of power would be extended over all the nations (specifically over Israel's enemies), and justice, order, and peace would be achieved throughout the realm (see Ps 101).

Jesus proclaims that this moment, the moment of God's intervention, his "coming to reign," is about to begin.

That is why his message is both good news and a call for repentance. For man is never ready for God's coming. He can only be less unprepared. And Jesus is calling for a decision that would be a "turning back" (the radical meaning of "repent") in order to experience God's reign precisely as *good* news. Inasmuch, however, as the reign is not yet visible but only imminent, the good news can presently be experienced only through faith: "*Believe* the good news." This formula is really addressed to Christians of *all* times—and therefore to us. For we cannot experience the kingdom as good for us unless we undergo a change of heart. And the announcement of the kingdom is not the fullness of it; it is not yet here. For the time being we have only signs of its beginning and not the kind of blinding light that removes any need for faith.

It would seem, from our examination of this text, that the person of Jesus is less important than the coming kingdom of which he is the herald. However, as we shall soon see, the message is not really distinct from the herald. For the kingdom begins to break in not as a big-bang moment *after* Jesus but as an invitation in and through what Jesus himself does. So God's blueprint for the world is not simply a repentance from sin and return to the covenant law. It is an act of belief in God's new action in the world, his "good news." And that good news is Jesus himself.

There is more: the response to Jesus changes people's lives and creates a community of disciples. To this development we turn next.

5

Fishers of Men

1:16-20

¹⁶And passing along by the Sea of Galilee, he saw Simon and Andrew the brother of Simon casting a net in the sea; for they were fishermen. ¹⁷And Jesus said to them, "Follow me and I will make you become fishers of men." ¹⁸And immediately they left their nets and followed him. ¹⁹And going on a little farther, he saw James the son of Zebedee and John his brother, who were in their boat mending the nets. ²⁰And immediately he called them; and they left their father Zebedee in the boat with the hired servants, and followed him.

WHY IS IT important for Mark to relate that the first action of Jesus, after announcing the kingdom, is to call disciples to follow him? If the kingdom were so imminent and the inbreaking of God's rule so close at hand, why was it not sufficient for Jesus simply to state that fact, trusting that the news would spread by word of mouth to all of Israel?

Obviously there is some kind of interim envisaged by Jesus and underlined by Mark. This is the period of discipleship, community, and mission. Hereafter Jesus will not be alone. He will be forming and instructing a band of followers who (as we know from 3:13) are to be with him and to be sent forth to preach.

The very brevity of Mark's account suggests the hurriedness and urgency of the call. Mark gives no psychological preparation of the disciples (as Lk 5:1-11 does) to make their immediate response more understandable. Jesus calls and men answer without hesitation or question. What a compelling power they must have felt from his eyes and his voice! They were fishermen, and it takes a mighty force to pull a fisherman away from what he has known all his life—his sea, his boat, his nets, his family, the security of knowing what to do next—to throw in his lot with this man who talks about God's kingdom.

"Fishers of men" is not just a play on words. In the Old Testament, God's coming intervention in judgment is described as his fishing with net or hook (Am 4:2; Hb 1:14-17; Jer 16:16; Ez 29:4-5; 38:4). The hour has come for God's fishing. The disciples, like Jesus, will gather men for God's judgment, which Jesus and Mark understand as a judgment of salvation for those who believe the good news (16:15). To what extent the disciples caught the scriptural allusions when Jesus first used them we don't know. All we know is that the call was compelling.

There are several lessons about discipleship introduced here. To learn in Jesus' school is first of all to follow him. The disciples learn the lessons of Jesus by living with him. He will teach them by word, of course, but only occasionally. He will teach them by his example at every moment. Christian education, as done by Jesus, is no mere head-trip! It is a lived experience. Secondly, there is no address for Jesus' school, no fixed place where the disciples gather daily to be taught. Jesus is constantly on the move. Discipleship is a journey.

Thirdly, Jesus provides no map to tell his disciples where they will be tomorrow. Discipleship is following Jesus wherever he decides to go *now*. It is to give Jesus control of the journey.

Fourthly, there is also an implication to be seen only later: To follow Jesus is to find oneself in the company of others not of one's own choosing. It is Jesus who calls, Jesus who chooses. And it should cause little surprise if the disciple, who can appreciate Jesus' wisdom in calling *him*, cannot readily appreciate the Master's wisdom in calling that *other*. The gospel of Mark itself shows that there will be much to be worked out between disciple and disciple before they come to the salt of divine wisdom that will put them at peace and make them servants of one another (cf. Mk 9:33-36, 50; 10:35-45).

Perhaps some of this still unfinished work is implied in

Jesus' saying, "I *will* make you *become* fishers of men." Nowhere in Mark is the disciples' journey ever ended, not even in Jerusalem, for after the resurrection they are to take the road back to Galilee (16:7).

Finally, there are those nets and things. The disciple cannot take with him anything but himself. It is as if Jesus were saying to the disciples of Mark's day and of ours: "Come—yes, come just as you are—but those nets have got to go."

6

A New Teaching with Authority

1:21-28

²¹And they went into Capernaum; and immediately on the sabbath he entered the synagogue and taught. ²²And they were astonished at his teaching, for he taught them as one who had authority, and not as the scribes. ²³And immediately there was in their synagogue a man with an unclean spirit; ²⁴and he cried out, "What have you to do with us, Jesus of Nazareth? Have you come to destroy us? I know who you are, the Holy One of God." ²⁵But Jesus rebuked him, saying, "Be silent, and come out of him!" ²⁶And the unclean spirit, convulsing him and crying with a loud voice, came out of him. ²⁷And they were all amazed, so that they questioned among themselves, saying, "What is this? A new teaching! With authority he commands even the unclean spirits, and they obey him." ²⁸And at once his fame spread everywhere throughout all the surrounding region of Galilee.

WITH A HANDFUL of picked disciples around him, Jesus, who has been *preaching* the kingdom, now begins to *teach*. There is a slight difference in meaning between the two words, the first emphasizing the announcement of an event, the second a more lengthy and relaxed unfolding of a discourse. For teaching Jesus begins by using the sabbath synagogue service as the occasion. He thus shows his message to be built on the scriptures and the piety of the Old Testament.

Before proceeding, first a word about Mark's frequent expression, "immediately." This is simply a characteristic of Mark's style (a carry-over from the oral stage of the gospel?), appearing so often it should not be pressed any more than a Canadian's tendency to end his statements with "eh?" It does, however, give the impression of haste to Mark's narrative.

The surprise created by Jesus' teaching is its authority (Greek, *exousia*). Because Mark contrasts Jesus' teaching with that of the scribes, some commentators think Mark is referring to Jesus' speaking the word of God directly (as, for example, in the Sermon on the Mount, "Moses said . . . But I say . . ."), whereas the scribes were accustomed to cite a genealogy of rabbinic interpretations when they taught. On the other hand, direct teaching by the rabbis was not unknown, and Jesus elsewhere occasionally uses rabbinic methods. Furthermore, Mark gives here no indication of the content of Jesus' preaching, as Matthew does in the Sermon on the Mount, all of which Matthew inserts into his gospel, concluding with the note of astonishment at Jesus' teaching which we have here in Mark. Matthew wants to explain the astonishment, in other words, in terms of the content of the teaching.

Not so Mark. He is interested in the *effect* of Jesus' teaching, and the story of the exorcism is used to explain just what Mark means by Jesus' *authority*. When Jesus teaches, things happen! His teaching is not just wisdom but power. The crowd calls the exorcism a teaching: "What is this? A new teaching! With authority he commands even the unclean spirits and they obey him!"

This is the first public encounter of Jesus with a demon since the temptation in the desert. As his first public work, it gives a key to the rest of Jesus' ministry, which will be a conflict with the powers of darkness. But it is also significant that Jesus performs this exorcism in the synagogue. The word "unclean" means unfit for worship. By his *teaching* with authority, Jesus renders not only the man but also the synagogue fit for worship. Later Jesus will cleanse the temple (11:15-18). While not an exorcism, the cleansing does have the effect of restoring the place to a house of prayer, and the crowds there, as here, call the action a *teaching*. For the Jewish leaders the cleansing of the temple raises again the question of Jesus' *authority* (11:28).

Therefore we can conclude that as a result of Jesus' teaching, the two places of Jewish worship were cleansed: the synagogue and the temple. Jesus teaches primarily by action.

The important question of Jesus' identity is once again raised by the response of the unclean spirit: "You are the holy one of God!" At this point, the supernatural powers recognize more in Jesus than do the crowds or the authorities or the disciples. Jesus is the "holy one of God," the bearer of the Holy Spirit. The demon is trying to fend off Jesus' superior power by naming him. The naming is successful, but the fending off is not. Elsewhere demons identify Jesus as "the Son of God" (3:11) and "Son of the Most High God" (5:7). Mark has already told us, in the opening of his gospel (1:1), that Jesus is the Son of God. But on the plane of human history, for the moment, only the demons recognize him for who he is. For the crowds and for the disciples, it will take a long pedagogy. Nevertheless, Jesus has begun to manifest his power, and people begin to wonder.

For Jesus, to teach is not only to speak God's word in the human void. It is to silence the noise, the disturbance, and the alienation wrought by the evil one. The rest of the gospel will continue this twofold dimension of Jesus' teaching.

7

A Healing Service—
What to Do with Success

1:29-39

²⁹And immediately, he left the synagogue, and entered the house of Simon and Andrew, with James and John. ³⁰Now Simon's mother-in-law lay sick with a fever, and immediately they told him of her. ³¹And he came and took her by the hand and lifted her up, and the fever left her; and she served them.

³²That evening, at sundown, they brought to him all who were sick or possessed with demons. ³³And the whole city was gathered together about the door. ³⁴And he healed many who were sick with various diseases, and cast out many demons; and he would not permit the demons to speak, because they knew him.

³⁵And in the morning, a great while before day, he rose and went out to a lonely place, and there he prayed. ³⁶And Simon and those who were with him followed him, ³⁷and they found him and said to him, "Every one is searching for you." ³⁸And he said to them, "Let us go on to the next towns, that I may preach there also; for that is why I came out." ³⁹And he went throughout all Galilee, preaching in their synagogues and casting out demons.

AFTER THE NOISY, crowd-awing exorcism in the synagogue, Jesus' first healing is a quiet and gentle contrast. Done on the same sabbath day (thus for Mark being, with the exorcism, a sample of the great works to come), the healing is more intimate and "ordinary." Jesus' name is not even used, and the story is as brief as possible; but his power and charm are felt as much in this domestic need as in the powerful public exorcism.

Mark is relating this story probably because it was part of a cluster of events narrated originally by Peter about an early day of the ministry in Capernaum. But it is also likely that Mark wants to teach something by repeating the information that the four initial disciples were with Jesus for this cure. Simon Peter and Andrew, of course, were kin. But what about James and John? The teaching for them as well as for the Christian reader seems to be connected with the note that as an effect of the healing "she served them." The surface meaning is probably that she got the evening meal. But if, as is likely, Mark intends the woman to be a typical disciple, he is hinting that the Christian is one who has been healed by Jesus and empowered by that healing to serve the community of Jesus' disciples. Later on in the gospel, the point will be made that greatness in the kingdom is to be measured by service (9:33-35). Now it is James and John who have to learn the lesson of service most of all (10:35-45). To one who knows the rest of the gospel, this meaning of the healing (i.e., its fruit in spontaneous service) can thus be seen. But the disciples will need the healing of their own blindness before they can understand that the greatest in the kingdom, Jesus, is the servant of all.

The crowds know that Jesus is at Peter's house, but as good Jews they wait until sunset has closed the sabbath before bringing the sick for Jesus to cure. "The whole town" is outside the door. Jesus heals and delivers (Mark clearly distinguishes again between the two activities), and he also muzzles the demons. Why? Beyond the reasons we suggested when commenting on the demoniac's cry in the synagogue, we might note Mark's reason here: "because they knew him." That is, the demons had a supernatural knowledge; it is not a confession of faith. Jesus does not want to be publicly identified by those who already *know* who he is. He wants rather a confession of faith by those who witness his works and teaching.

There is the color of a personal reminiscence in the next scene. Though the night healing service was long, Jesus is up before daybreak to pray. He has withdrawn from his disciples, and the tone of reproach in their exclamation when they find him suggests that the success story so important to them is less important to Jesus, who cannot forget the real reason why he has come—to proclaim the Father's kingdom and to do cosmic battle with the evil one. The stage on which Jesus is operating is really that desert place where he first encountered Satan. There is no desert around Capernaum. Mark's meaning is that the "lonely" place to which Jesus withdrew symbolized his return to the desert, a reminder to the Christian reader that something much more cosmic is in the offing than simply the wonderful signs of the night before. When Jesus rejoins his disciples it is not to return to the applause of Capernaum. For the moment the people of Simon's town have had sufficient signs of the inbreaking of the kingdom. Jesus pushes on throughout Galilee, proclaiming his message and dispossessing the demonic powers.

There is an admirable freedom and sense of mission about Jesus in this text. He does not cling to the place of his greatest missionary success. He plunges into yet unclaimed and uncharted territory. To do otherwise would be to fall victim to the tempter, who sometimes uses success to "settle" those God calls to be "unsettled" pioneers. Jesus will eventually go to the cross because he refused to "settle" for anything less than God's complete will.

8

Jesus Cures a Leper

1:40-45

⁴⁰And a leper came to him beseeching him, and kneeling said to him, "If you will, you can make me clean." ⁴¹Moved with pity, he stretched out his hand and

touched him, and said to him, "I will; be clean." ⁴²And immediately the leprosy left him, and he was made clean. ⁴³And he sternly charged him, and sent him away at once, ⁴⁴and said to him, "See that you say nothing to any one; but go, show yourself to the priest, and offer for your cleansing what Moses commanded, for a proof to the people." ⁴⁵But he went out and began to talk freely about it, and to spread the news, so that Jesus could no longer openly enter a town, but was out in the country; and people came to him from every quarter.

MARK CONCLUDES HIS account of Jesus' preaching tour of the villages in Galilee with the story of a healing. Though it is not an exorcism, Mark relates it in such a way as to indicate that it is not just an act of mercy but another victorious clash of Jesus with the powers of evil and death.

"Leprosy" in the Bible covers a variety of skin diseases. The mandate of Leviticus 13:45-46 required lepers to wear torn clothes, to let their hair hang loose, to cry "Unclean! Unclean!" and to live outside the camp. They were, however, allowed to attend synagogue services behind a protective screen. It is thus possible that Jesus encountered the man in one of the synagogues. At any rate, what is amazing is the daring faith of the leper. He risks approaching Jesus, facing a possible rejection at least by the crowds. Mark gives us no idea who the leper thinks Jesus is—he uses no title to address him. But he has no doubt of his sovereign power. To cure the leper all Jesus has to do is to will it.

What is Jesus' reaction? Here there is a textual problem. Some Greek manuscripts, followed by most of our English translations, read, "Moved with pity" (or the equivalent), while others of the so-called Western tradition read, "Becoming angry." A good case can be made for the latter translation, because we could easily understand how a scribe would have been offended by the idea of Jesus' becoming angry before a cure and would have softened the idea to conform with other places in the gospels where Jesus is shown to react with pity.

The reverse procedure would be hard to imagine. If "becoming angry" is the original, however paradoxical it may seem, it tells us much about Mark's view of Jesus. Confronted with the evil of sickness, Jesus' first reaction is a flash of anger—not at the man but at the physical evil by which he is bound. Jesus' reaction here, then, would be the same as his reaction upon finding vendors in the temple. The place of God's dwelling needs to be cleansed!

Jesus does more than will the cleansing, however. He actually touches the leper, matching the leper's risk by a risk of his own, for to touch a leper was to automatically incur ritual uncleanness. Jesus spurns a ritual prohibition in order to meet the leper as he is—in his leprosy! This kind of behavior will soon get Jesus into trouble, but it is consistent with the picture given by each of the gospels. Jesus *enters* man's sick and sinful world. Where the self-righteous will not go, lest they be stained, Jesus goes with the power to heal.

Then Jesus "sternly charged him and sent him away at once." At this point in his ministry, as the sequence shows, publicity about the cure could block Jesus' mission of synagogue preaching. We don't know whether the leper went to the priest or not, but he did disobey Jesus' command to keep it quiet, with the result that Jesus was beginning to be hailed more as a healer than as a synagogue preacher. People were paying more attention to his cures than to his words.

In Mark's view, this was not Jesus' intention, but Jesus adapted his methods to the development of events over which he himself was not in total control. We are being alerted already now to the fact that the course of Jesus' life is being laid out by someone other than himself—a course that will ultimately lead Jesus to a personal fate he had not planned, the cross. But that meeting with the cross was the mysterious result of the good he could not help doing for the sick despite the taboos of the legalists. Mark will now demonstrate the same development in five conflicts of Jesus with his enemies.

The possibility of that conflict has already been hinted at in the expression, "as a witness to them." The *them* is probably not the people but the priests, who will have to face the fact that what was recorded only twice in the Old Testament (Nm 12:10-15; 2 Kgs 5:1-14), and what rabbinical tradition considered to be as difficult as raising the dead—namely, the healing of a leper—has happened at the touch of Jesus of Nazareth.

9

Jesus and the Paralytic

2:1-12

2 And when he returned to Capernaum after some days, it was reported that he was at home. [2]And many were gathered together, so that there was no longer room for them, not even about the door; and he was preaching the word to them. [3]And they came, bringing to him a paralytic carried by four men. [4]And when they could not get near him because of the crowd, they removed the roof above him; and when they had made an opening, they let down the pallet on which the paralytic lay. [5]And when Jesus saw their faith, he said to the paralytic, "My son, your sins are forgiven." [6]Now some of the scribes were sitting there, questioning in their hearts, [7]"Why does this man speak thus? It is blasphemy! Who can forgive sins but God alone?" [8]And immediately Jesus, perceiving in his spirit that they thus questioned within themselves, said to them, "Why do you question thus in your hearts? [9]Which is easier, to say to the paralytic, 'Your sins are forgiven,' or to say, 'Rise, take up your pallet and walk'? [10]But that you may know that the Son of man has authority on earth to forgive sins"—he said to the paralytic—[11]"I say to you, rise, take up your pallet and go home." [12]And he rose, and immediately took up the pallet and went out before them all; so that they were

all amazed and glorified God, saying, "We never saw anything like this!"

WITH THE HEALING of the paralytic begins a series of five events, each of which brings Jesus into mounting conflict, climaxing in the plot of Jesus' enemies to destroy him (3:6). This series of encounters in Galilee prepares us for a similar series of five conflicts with the authorities in Jerusalem (11:27-12:37). But each story has a lesson in its own right too.

Jesus is back "at home" in Capernaum—at Peter's house, we may assume. Though he has not the space either of synagogue or town square, he preaches "the word" to those who gather. Note how Mark uses "the word" without qualification, as he will do again in 4:14-20. There it is the message about the kingdom, told to the crowds in parables and explained privately to his disciples. "The word" by Mark's day had already become a technical term for the gospel.

It is well known in town by now that when Jesus teaches, things happen (1:21-28). And so four friends rush a paralytic to the house where Jesus is preaching. Finding the door blocked with the crowds, they climb the ladder to the roof and break a hole in it. We can imagine Simon Peter's reaction, living as he did in a culture that knew nothing of insurance!

It is the faith of the four friends, rather than that of the paralytic that wins Jesus' attention—a lesson about community and about intercession for those too paralyzed to speak for themselves! Jesus' first word may seem to us of modern culture irrelevant. Why doesn't he heal the man first? For the simple reason that he goes to the root of the man's being: his alienation from God and the burden of his guilt. Though it is not said that the man's paralysis is due to his personal sins, the relationship between sin and sickness, between reconciliation and health was so strong in Old Testament tradition that "healing" and "forgiveness" were often interchangeable terms (Ps 41:4; Jer 3:22; Hos 14:4). The fact that the man does not rise immediately upon the word of forgiveness shows that healing is more than forgiveness. But it also shows that forgiveness is the door to healing.

The shock of Jesus' statement lies in his claim to speak for God, since only God can forgive sins. While the words hardly go beyond Nathan's declaration to David that his sin was forgiven (2 Sm 12:13), the scribes rightly suspect what the Christian reader knows to be true: Jesus is actually forgiving in God's name. They accuse Jesus of blasphemy—if only in their hearts.

Jesus, reading their hearts (and thus further showing his divine credentials), takes up the challenge. He confronts them with a question. From the viewpoint of their theology, it is obviously more difficult to forgive sins than to restore a paralytic. But from the viewpoint of a visible sign, it is easier to say, "Your sins are forgiven," since only God would know whether this forgiveness really took place. However, if the prophet says, "Arise and walk," all the bystanders would know by simple observation whether the word was effective or not. Now if the two words issue from the same mouth and the lame man actually walks, this would be a confirming sign that the forgiveness was as real as the healing.

This is exactly what happens. The paralytic is restored not only to health but to his family and to the village. And—for the Christian who knows how to read the power of the Son of Man—the reason is that the man has been restored in the first place to God by Jesus' word.

The paralytic has experienced a resurrection: "Arise!" Jesus says. Many of the healings in Mark anticipate the resurrection. Jesus "lifted up" Peter's mother-in-law (1:31). To Jairus' daughter, thought to be dead, Jesus says, as he says to the paralytic, "Arise!" (5:41). Similarly, the epileptic boy is thought to be dead, "but Jesus took him by the hand and lifted him up, and he arose" (9:27). Of course, these are not resurrections in the sense of the final resurrection from the dead. They are, in the physical order, a raising up from sickness or at most resuscitation. But as signs of Jesus' power over sickness and even death itself, they could hardly have failed to be interpreted by the Christian readers of Mark, and doubtless by Mark himself, as anticipations of the resurrection. Certainly they tell us what redemption means: forgiveness of sins and restoration of wholeness, both in one's physical being and in one's relationships.

Jesus, The Caller and Teacher of Sinners

2:13-17

[13]He went out again beside the sea; and all the crowd gathered about him, and he taught them. [14]And as he passed on, he saw Levi the son of Alphaeus sitting at the tax office, and he said to him, "Follow me." And he rose and followed him.

[15]And as he sat at table in his house, many tax collectors and sinners were sitting with Jesus and his disciples; for there were many who followed him. [16]And the scribes of the Pharisees, when they saw that he was eating with sinners and tax collectors, said to his disciples, "Why does he eat with tax collectors and sinners?" [17]And when Jesus heard it, he said to them, "Those who are well have no need of a physician, but those who are sick; I came not to call the righteous, but sinners."

THE TRANSITION FROM the cure of the paralytic to the call of Levi would be less complicated if Mark had simply omitted the opening verse about Jesus' first going again to the seashore, and a crowd gathering again. Matthew and Luke do in fact omit it, but for Mark the detail is important. Wherever Jesus goes—to the wilderness, to Peter's house, or to the seashore—he is besieged. Jesus does not pursue the crowd. On the contrary, after a mighty work he habitually withdraws to another arena.

But when the crowd gathers, he *teaches* them. This detail too is important for Mark. Earlier we saw how Jesus' teaching is new and different because, unlike the scribes and the Pharisees, he teaches with *authority*—that is, when Jesus teaches, things happen (1:22-27). Now we are about to see another way in which this teacher differs from the established teachers of the day: they avoid sinners; Jesus seeks them out.

The point is illustrated when Jesus calls a tax collector to follow him. As with the earlier call of the fishermen (1:16-20), this call is told with skeletal brevity. Levi may have known Jesus, and he surely knew Peter, but again there is no indication of any psychological preparation for the call. Jesus calls, Levi follows—as simple as that. Mark knows how to focus on the only adequate reason anyone would follow Jesus: "He called me."

But if fishing was a respectable profession, tax collecting was not. A tax collector could, for a price, buy a government license to tax and then gouge the people for as much profit as he could make. It is a small wonder that in Jewish practice tax collectors were not allowed to serve as judges nor to witness at court, nor even to attend the synagogue.

The amazing move of Jesus in calling this worst of social outcasts to the company of his disciples is heightened by the fact that "many" tax collectors and sinners followed Jesus, apparently in the wake of Levi, and that Jesus dines with them at Levi's house.

To appreciate what a shock this was to the "scribes of the Pharisees," we need to understand what is meant by "sinners" here and what it meant to eat with them. The Pharisees classified as "sinners" not only notorious criminals or people of disrepute but also the common people unlearned in the law. They reasoned as follows. In order to observe the whole law perfectly one had to know it. Since the common people were ignorant of the fine points of the law because they were unable to study it, they must transgress it frequently—and ignorance of the law was no excuse. Only the learned, therefore, could really be holy. Even the great rabbi Hillel said, "The common people cannot be pious." The Pharisees further reasoned that to associate with these common people to the extent of sharing a meal with them was to expose oneself to the danger of violating the laws of ritual purity. The safer course of avoidance then became the rule. This is how the name "Pharisees" came to be applied to this learned (and "holy") elite. It means "separated ones," separated, that is, from the common people unlearned in the law. Now while all the Pharisees aspired to know and practice the law, they looked to their scribes as specialists in teaching and interpreting the law. The scribes were the Pharisees' theologians. Jesus, the new teacher, by what he does as much as by what he says, flies in the face of this establishment.

The objection they raise is not yet an open accusation, but it is stronger than "thinking in their hearts," as in the preceding story of the paralytic. Here they speak to Jesus' disciples. But Jesus hears their complaint and counters with a pithy formulation of what he is teaching by example: "Those who are well have no need of a physician, but those who are sick. I came not to call the righteous but sinners."

The Pharisees are not really so righteous as they think they are, but their confidence in their spiritual health leads them to ignore the doctor in their midst. The tax collectors and sinners are the more obviously "sick," and they respond to Jesus' magnanimous wall-breaking with equal magnificence—a celebration! The whole account raises the question of who is really sick and who is well, who are the righteous and who the sinners. In the shocking initiative of Jesus and the equally surprising response of sinners and tax collectors, human categories get reversed. God is making a new people with a new kind of holiness. The raw material is not saints but sinners. And the heart of holiness is not knowledge or observance. It is table fellowship with Jesus.

11

On Feasting and Fasting

2:18-22

¹⁸Now John's disciples and the Pharisees were fasting; and people came and said to him, "Why do John's disciples and the disciples of the Pharisees fast, but your disciples do not fast? ¹⁹And Jesus said to them, "Can the wedding guests fast while the bridegroom is with them? As long as they have the bridegroom with them, they cannot fast. ²⁰The days will come, when the bridegroom is taken away from them, and then they will fast in that day. ²¹No one sews a piece of unshrunk cloth on an old garment; if he does, the patch tears away from it, the new from the old, and a worse tear is made. ²²And no one puts new wine into old wineskins; if he does, the wine will burst the skins, and the wine is lost, and so are the skins; but new wine is for fresh skins."

THERE ARE THREE levels at which this story can be understood. At the level of Mark's composition, it is the third of a mounting series of conflicts between Jesus and his critics in Galilee. At the level of Mark's community, it preserves sayings of Jesus important for the community's life and practice, particularly in the matter of fasting. At the level of Jesus' original ministry, it contains an important statement of how Jesus' ministry is new and different even from that of John the Baptist.

In Old Testament times people fasted to show their repentance (Jon 3:5), to atone for their sins (Lv 16:29; 23:26-32; Nm 29:7), to mourn a personal or national tragedy (1 Sm 31:13), or to intercede with prayer for some important need, personal (2 Sm 12:16-17) or collective (Jl 1:14). Daniel fasted that he might understand the scriptures (Dn 9:1-27). Fasting was thought to be especially appropriate for widows as a sign of mourning the absence of their husbands, but also perhaps because increasingly the holy and prayerful widow was seen as a symbol of the whole people longing for reunion with the Lord, or for the coming of his kingdom (Jd 8:6; Anna, Lk 2:37).

Was it this that prompted the Pharisees to fast twice a week (Lk 18:12), or was it to express their religious consecration? We can't be certain, but it is likely that John's disciples fasted to prepare themselves for the coming of the kingdom (understood primarily as judgment) and perhaps to hasten its arrival.

Jesus' counter-question to John's disciples makes clear that Jesus is not just a pointer to the kingdom as John was, a "voice" in the wilderness (Mk 1:3; Jn 1:23). Jesus may herald the kingdom, but it is also already begun in him. Now is the time for joy and celebration, says Jesus. Just as one would not think of fasting at a wedding feast, Jesus' disciples should not think of fasting with Jesus in their midst.

Is Jesus merely using a comparison to illustrate the joy appropriate for the time of his ministry, or is he actually claiming to be the bridegroom of the new people of God? Nowhere in the Old Testament was the Messiah spoken of as the bridegroom of the people—only the Lord himself could be that. If Jesus were actually claiming to be the bridegroom in that sense, it would have caused amazement among the people and perhaps even the accusation of blasphemy. Here is a good example of how Jesus' words could have a simple and direct meaning to the Jewish listener, and yet come to mean something much more to the Christian community in the light of what it knew of the whole gospel, climaxing in the resurrection. The Jewish listener may have understood simply: "Now is the time for joy." But the Christian reader of Mark knows that the bridegroom is indeed Jesus himself (cf. 2 Cor 11:2; Eph 5:23; Rv 19:7; 21:2; Jn 3:29).

"The days will come, when the bridegroom is taken away from them" is a veiled allusion to Jesus' death. The fasting of John's disciples may have been, in addition to a preparation for the kingdom, an expression of mourning the loss of their master at Herod's violent hands. At any rate, the text of Mark tells us the reason for Christian fasting in the period after Jesus' death and resurrection. It is a longing for the return of Jesus. As the bride anxiously awaits the arrival of her husband, so the church fasts out of longing to see Jesus again.

The last two sayings about patches and wineskins simply illustrate in other ways what Jesus has said in the image of the wedding feast: With Jesus there is an entirely new situation present, calling for new categories of thought and behavior. Jesus' disciples cannot fast now because, unlike the Pharisees and even unlike John's disciples, they are not focusing on an ascetical practice nor on the judgment about to come but instead are rejoicing in the salvation already present in Jesus.

The church ever since has perceived the tension of the two rhythms and celebrated them. She knows Jesus as present and so she feasts. She knows Jesus as coming and so she fasts.

12

Lord of the Sabbath

2:23-28

²³One sabbath he was going through the grainfields; and as they made their way his disciples began to pluck ears of grain. ²⁴And the Pharisees said to him, "Look, why are they doing what is not lawful on the sabbath?" ²⁵And he said to them, "Have you never read what David did, when he was in need and was hungry, he and those who were with him: ²⁶how he entered the house of God, when Abiathar was high priest, and ate the bread of the Presence, which it is not lawful for any but the priests to eat, and also gave it to those who were with him?" ²⁷And he said to them,

"The sabbath was made for man, not man for the sabbath; [28]so the Son of man is lord even of the sabbath."

THE FOURTH CONFLICT in this series tells us how Jesus understands the meaning of law; but it goes beyond this to tell us in
a new way who Jesus is.

In the course of a sabbath walk, Jesus' disciples pluck heads
of grain, rub them free of the husks, and eat. For a passerby or
a neighbor to do such a thing was quite acceptable practice and
sanctioned by the law, as long as one did not put a sickle to the
grain (Dt 23:25). The purpose of the allowance was a humane
consideration for those who might be hungry. The Pharisees,
however, interpret the action as reaping, forbidden on the sabbath (Ex 34:21). Assuming rightly that Jesus sanctioned his disciples' action, they ask him why he permits them to do this.

Jesus answers with an example of human understanding of
the law. When David and his men needed food, they were
given the holy bread from the sanctuary when there was none
other to eat.

In the text of 1 Samuel 21:1-6, the priest who provides the
showbread is not Abiathar, as Mark has it, but his father,
Ahimelech. How are we to explain the discrepancy in Mark? It
could, of course, just be the error of a scribe copying the text.
But other explanations are more persuasive. The Hebrew text
of 2 Samuel 8:17 names Abiathar as the father, not the son, of
Ahimelech. So there was some confusion of names even in the
Old Testament tradition, and Jesus may just have been following the tradition current in his day.

Still another explanation is possible. The Greek of Mark
reads literally, "how he entered the house of God *about Abiathar the high priest."* It is exactly the same construction we find
in Mark 12:26, "Have you not read in the book of Moses *about
the bush"*—meaning, as the Revised Standard Version correctly
interprets, *"in the passage about* the bush." In either case Jesus
would be referring to the *general location* of the passage in the
Old Testament scroll rather than to a specific time. Now Abiathar *is* mentioned in the general section to which Jesus is refer-

ring (1 Sm 22:20). And Abiathar was better known as the high priest during David's reign (2 Sm 20:25).

The difficulties of this text (of which Matthew and Luke are apparently aware, since they omit the reference to Abiathar) must not be brushed aside. But neither does our salvation depend on the accuracy of this detail or the complete agreement of all the biblical texts. It was the awareness of such occasional textual disagreements that led the Second Vatican Council to clarify in what sense and for what purpose the scriptures are inspired by the Holy Spirit:

> Since everything asserted by the inspired authors or sacred writers must be held to be asserted by the Holy Spirit, it follows that the books of scripture must be acknowledged as teaching solidly, faithfully, and without error that truth God wanted put into sacred writings *for the sake of salvation (Dei Verbum,* 11).

The point being made for our salvation here is not who happened to be high priest. The point is that the sabbath is made for man to rejoice in and enjoy. It is not for his strangulation. The Pharisees were so bent on getting mathematical certitude about their justification that they could no longer see that the original purpose of the sabbath law, as Deuteronomy made clear, was to enable man to be less a work animal and more a human being, rejoicing in his freedom from slavery by God's gift. To become enslaved by a law of freedom is irony indeed.

Up to this point one might conclude that Jesus has merely outwitted the Pharisees by displaying a more humane interpretation of the sabbath law, as a wiser rabbi might. But for Mark, Jesus is not merely the wisest of rabbis. He is the Son of Man who is Lord of the sabbath. That means that he has the authority to legislate in his own right about the sabbath.

It is hard for us at this distance to appreciate what a revolutionary statement this was. The basic issue, Mark is telling us, is not whether you may pluck the grain of a field you walk through on the sabbath. The basic issue is who Jesus is. A new consciousness has dawned upon the Christian community: What now holds is not the old law as such but only Jesus' interpretation of it. And Jesus' authority to interpret derives not from a rabbinical wisdom but from who he is—the Son of Man who is Lord of the sabbath.

13

To Save Life or To Kill?

3:1-6

3 Again he entered the synagogue, and a man was there who had a withered hand. ²And they watched him, to see whether he would heal him on the sabbath, so that they might accuse him. ³And he said to the man who had the withered hand, "Come here." ⁴And he said to them, "Is it lawful on the sabbath to do good or to do harm, to save life or to kill?" But they were silent. ⁵And he looked around at them with anger, grieved at their hardness of heart, and said to the man, "Stretch out your hand." He stretched it out, and his hand was restored. ⁶The Pharisees went out, and immediately held counsel with the Herodians against him, how to destroy him.

INITIALLY, THE CURE of the man with the withered hand appears to be just another marvelous healing. But in Mark's journal it is much more than that. Done on a sabbath, it is an illustration of Jesus' claim to be Lord of the sabbath. It is also the climax of a series of five mounting conflicts between Jesus and his enemies in Galilee.

In the first of these conflicts, the healing of the paralytic, the scribes question Jesus' authority but do so only in their hearts, not daring to challenge him openly (2:7). In the second, they question Jesus' *disciples* about his consorting with tax collectors and sinners (2:16). In the third, questioners address Jesus himself (2:18). In the fourth, the Pharisees openly accuse Jesus and his disciples of violating the sabbath (3:2). Now, climactically, it is Jesus who takes the initiative, carrying the conflict into his enemies' camp by a question. Finally beaten in oral conflict, they plot to destroy him.

The story, then, is more about the authority of Jesus than about the cure of a withered hand. Scribal tradition permitted the practice of medicine and healing on the sabbath only if there was danger to life. Obviously, every healing Jesus worked—and certainly this one—could have waited a day without danger to life. This, at least, is what his adversaries thought.

But Jesus thinks differently. He calls the man forward to the center of the crowd as one would call a witness to the stand. Then he puts to his opponents an either-or question that brushes legality aside and makes the situation a life-or-death issue to be resolved at this very moment: "Is it lawful on the sabbath to do good or to do harm, to save life or to kill?"

The question is met with stoney silence. Jesus then "looks around at them with anger." The Greek suggests that Jesus slowly circled the crowd, looking into the eye of each person. Here we meet Jesus' anger again. In the light of so many New Testament texts about the dangers of anger, this one must be acknowledged as an important witness to the fact that anger, indignation, and outrage can be holy, and that there are occasions where anger is the only Christian response. Yet Jesus' anger is tempered by sadness at the hardness of heart of those who would hold back the gift of life from a brother Israelite. Jesus will weep over Jerusalem for the same reason.

Jesus wants the healing to be as obvious as the question. There is no secrecy about it, no command to keep it quiet. Instead, Jesus tells the man to stretch out his hand so that all may see life being given before their very eyes. (The raising of Lazarus, the last of Jesus' "signs" in John's gospel serves a similar public function.)

And so it happens. The Pharisees are defeated in the fifth

round. From debate they turn to action, teaming up with the supporters of Herod Antipas, the political power of Galilee, to destroy Jesus. Ironically, in the sabbath debate over life and death, Jesus chooses to give life. His enemies, however, choose to deal death to the life-giver. They unconsciously illustrate their response to Jesus' question: Is it lawful on the sabbath to do good or to do harm, to save life or to kill?

The shadow of the cross has thus fallen starkly over this bright page of miracles. The ominous last line not only closes the series of conflicts; it tells us that the section from 1:14 to this point is the whole gospel in miniature. Jesus preaches and heals and acts in a way that shows he has a divine authority. He is "Lord of the sabbath." This kind of teaching and acting, and this sort of claim, will lead ultimately to his own destruction. We will not be surprised to see the same theme running through a similar series of five conflicts in Jerusalem, where the murder of the Son is likewise foretold (12:6-7) and shortly thereafter fulfilled on Calvary.

14

Brighter Light, Darker Shadows
3:7-19

⁷Jesus withdrew with his disciples to the sea, and a great multitude from Galilee followed; also from Judea ⁸and Jerusalem and Idumea and from beyond the Jordan and from about Tyre and Sidon a great multitude, hearing all that he did, came to him. ⁹And he told his disciples to have a boat ready for him because of the crowd, lest they should crush him; ¹⁰for he had healed many, so that all who had diseases pressed upon him to touch him. ¹¹And whenever the unclean spirits be-

held him, they fell down before him and cried out, "You are the Son of God." [12]And he strictly ordered them not to make him known.

[13]And he went up into the hills, and called to him those whom he desired; and they came to him. [14]And he appointed twelve, to be with him, and to be sent out to preach [15]and have authority to cast out demons: [16]Simon whom he surnamed Peter; [17]James the son of Zebedee and John the brother of James, whom he surnamed Boanerges, that is, sons of thunder; [18]Andrew, and Philip, and Bartholomew, and Matthew, and Thomas, and James the son of Alphaeus, and Thaddaeus, and Simon the Cananaean, [19]and Judas Iscariot, who betrayed him.

THE SECTION BEGINNING here and running through 6:13 continues the report of Jesus' ministry in Galilee, but tells us of new developments. Out of the many disciples and hangers-on Jesus selects twelve (3:13-19) and eventually sends them forth on mission (6:6-13). Between these two references to the Twelve, Jesus experiences open rejection both by the scribes and by his own townspeople. Yet even in the hostile environment he continues to teach through parables and to manifest his divine power, now more amazingly than before. In addition to another exorcism (5:1-20) and a healing (5:25-34), Jesus shows his power over the chaotic forces of nature (4:35-41) and even raises the dead to life (5:35-43).

The lines are thus being drawn ever more clearly, not only between Jesus and the powers of evil, and not only between Jesus and his human enemies, but also between disciples who are committed and worthy of trust and those half-hearted enthusiasts who cannot decide between Jesus and the world (4:13-20). The reader of the gospel is subtly but powerfully being challenged to a similar decision.

Mark prefaces this long section by reporting that Jesus withdrew from the synagogue again to the sea—the theater to which he withdrew once before (2:13). This is where the action of most of this section will be localized. By this time Jesus' fame has spread not only to Jerusalem but to all the areas surrounding the Holy Land—each of which Jesus will eventually visit, with the exception of Idumea in the extreme south.

It is primarily his healing power that draws the crowds. Some scholars say that Mark is making a negative judgment here, implying that the crowds are drawn for selfish reasons. True, Jesus is more than a healer, and those he calls to be his disciples must learn what that more is. But Jesus accepts the crowds as they are, in their need, and heals the sick. A pattern for evangelization is revealed here.

Again Jesus is confronted with the untimely confession by the demons. They know his true identity. Whether their confession "You are the Son of God" is an attempt to gain power over Jesus by naming him (according to the magical belief of the ancient world that to name a mysterious power is to control it), or whether this is an admission of Jesus' superior authority (more likely, in view of their falling down before him), their confession is not a confession of loving and trusting faith. It is not the confession Jesus is looking for. That confession will be made appropriately only by believers, and it will happen only after Jesus dies on the cross.

Suddenly the scene switches from the sea to "the mountain," the traditional place of God's revelation since the Exodus from Egypt. Here Jesus calls and appoints the Twelve. This call differs from the call of the first disciples (1:16-20; 2:14) in two important ways. First, in the number twelve. This is an official constitution of a body of intimate disciples who will hereafter be with Jesus throughout his ministry—Mark will mention them nine more times in his gospel. Why twelve? Not because twelve is an ideal number for group dynamics but rather because the number echoes the twelve patriarchs of the twelve tribes of Israel and points forward to the upcoming creation of the new Israel. However much liberal scholars may claim that Jesus thought the end of time was so close that he could not have founded a church, we have here an obvious commitment on his part to the fashioning of a people, the new Israel, with new leaders. Certainly this is Mark's view of the events.

Secondly, the twofold purpose of the call is given: to be with him and to be sent out on mission. Both elements are important. We could have surmised the first from the earlier scenes where Jesus has called men to follow him. But here it is an explicit foundational principle: Those who proclaim and witness the good news must first experience it in the person of Jesus. The missionary never ceases to be a disciple. The second element is entirely new, for this is the first mention of a mission to be given to the disciples. Jesus will actually send them out at the end of this section (6:6-13).

Four of the Twelve listed here receive a special comment—Judas, for his betrayal, James and John, whom Jesus calls "sons of thunder" (probably because of their explosive temperaments), and Simon. Simon heads the list and is given the name Peter, "Cephas" in Aramaic, meaning "rock." In this context, it is not a proper name but a title, indicating Simon's call to be not only spokesman for the Twelve but also—if we take the rest of the gospel tradition into account—to be the foundation on which the new people of God will rest.

The kingdom on earth has begun to take clearer shape—but so have the powers of darkness. To their new confrontation we turn next.

15

The Spirit in Jesus— Jesus' New Family

3:19-35

¹⁹Then he went home; ²⁰and the crowd came together again, so that they could not even eat. ²¹And when his friends heard it, they went out to seize him, for they

said, "He is beside himself." [22]And the scribes who
came down from Jerusalem said, "He is possessed by
Beelzebul, and by the prince of demons he casts out
the demons." [23]And he called them to him, and said to
them in parables, "How can Satan cast out Satan? [24]If a
kingdom is divided against itself, that kindgom cannot
stand. [25]And if a house is divided against itself, that
house will not be able to stand. [26]And if Satan has risen
up against himself and is divided, he cannot stand, but
is coming to an end. [27]But no one can enter a strong
man's house and plunder his goods, unless he first
binds the strong man; then indeed he may plunder his
house.

[28]"Truly, I say to you, all sins will be forgiven the
sons of men, and whatever blasphemies they utter;
[29]but whoever blasphemes against the Holy Spirit never
has forgiveness, but is guilty of an eternal sin"—[30]for
they had said, "He has an unclean spirit."

[31]And his mother and his brothers came; and standing outside they sent to him and called him. [32]And a
crowd was sitting about him; and they said to him,
"Your mother and your brothers are outside, asking for
you." [33]And he replied, "Who are my mother and my
brothers?" [34]And looking around at those who sat
about him, he said, "Here are my mother and my
brothers! [35]Whoever does the will of God is my brother,
and sister, and mother."

JESUS AND THE twelve he has just chosen are now contrasted
with two, and possibly three, other groups. There is no doubt as
to the identity of the scribes in verses 22-27 and of the family of
Jesus in verses 31-35. The group in verse 21, however, is collo-
quially identified by Mark as "those by him"—which can mean
"family" (RSV, NAB, NEB), "relatives" (JB), "neighbors," "associates," or "friends" (AV). Is this the same group as "his
mother and his brothers," mentioned in verse 31? We can't be
sure. All we know is that it was a group, other than his intimate

disciples, whose negative response to Jesus Mark considered worth reporting. Theirs is not the kind of accusation the scribes will make. It appears to come from a concern about Jesus' mental health—and physical health, too, since they decide to move in when they see he no longer has time to eat. The "home" or "house" to which Jesus has gone is doubtless Peter's, Jesus' base for his Capernaum ministry. His "people" want to take him back to his hometown Nazareth for deprogramming.

By this time, however, Jesus' fame has reached the official ears of Jerusalem. A party of scribes, perhaps official investigators sent by the Sanhedrin, openly accuses him of being demon-possessed, saying his miracles are due to the power of "the prince of demons." Jesus responds with the logic of the obvious. His miracles and even his teaching have all resulted in the vanquishing of Satan's power. If it were by Satan that Jesus were working, then Satan would be destroying his own kingdom. Satan is indeed the strong man, but Jesus, whom the Baptist had hailed as the "stronger one" (1:7), has begun to bind him as a prelude to despoiling his house.

Then Jesus turns to the accusation that he is personally demon-possessed. This charge amounts to blasphemy, since it is equivalent to profaning the holy name of God. All sins, even blasphemy, can be forgiven, but not the sin of blasphemy against the Holy Spirit. What does this mean? Christian interpreters of this passage have reasoned as follows. Certainly the only sin that God could not forgive must be the sin for which one never asks forgiveness. Sinning against the light by deliberately calling evil good and good evil puts one on the likely path of final unrepentance. This is what the scribes are doing by accusing Jesus of being possessed by Beelzebul. It is a sin against the light. Mark himself underlines the specific and limited application of this principle to the present situation by his concluding line: "For they were saying, 'He has an unclean spirit.'"

Finally, this little section is rounded off by the appearance of the mother and the brothers of Jesus. While there is no doubt who the mother of Jesus is, the term "brothers" can cover varying degrees of relationship, as does the term "sisters," which we find added in some of the Greek manuscripts. They stand "outside." This can mean simply outside the house and on the fringe of the gathered crowd. If, however, they are the same group mentioned above who wished to seize Jesus as demented, Mark may also be suggesting a spiritual distance from Jesus as well. A message is passed to Jesus that they are "asking for" him. They have not come to listen as disciples but rather to get his attention.

Jesus' response means that there is a relationship with him more real and important than the physical, especially when the latter impedes the inbreaking kingdom of God. Looking around at those who sat about him—and Mark means primarily the Twelve—Jesus says that "whoever does the will of God is my brother, and sister, and mother." In Jesus' new family of the spirit, relationship to him is established not by blood but by one's surrender to God's will revealed in Jesus.

Christian piety is reluctant to accept the idea that the mother of Jesus could be associated with such a short-sighted view of his ministry, or that Jesus could have disdained his own mother's request in this fashion. It is not clear, of course, just how Mary was involved in this incident. Did she initiate it? Was she influenced by the others beyond her own preference? Was she persuaded to intercede because of the mounting danger which the Jerusalem scribes' investigation signaled? Or was it simply to Mark's advantage to mention Jesus' mother among his relatives in preparation for his statement concerning relationship to him? The text alone does not allow us to decide. The tradition here surely indicates lack of understanding on the part of Jesus' relatives, however well-intentioned they may have been. John 7:5 darkens this tradition with the words, "Even his brothers did not believe in him."

Yet this evidence must be balanced by the exceptional role of Mary's faith in the Cana episode in John's gospel as well as the fact that Luke holds her up repeatedly as a model of faith, discipleship, and doing the will of God (Lk 1:38, 45; 2:19, 51; 11:28). Luke also records her presence, and the presence of the brothers of Jesus, in the upper room, persevering in prayer (Acts 1:14). As far as Jesus' own teaching is concerned, he upholds the law of respect for parents: "'Honor your father and your mother'; and 'He who speaks evil of his father or mother, let him surely die'" (Mk 7:10).

How shall we then explain Jesus' words here? For a Jew, physical relationship was a high priority, and, while there were converts to Judaism, the first-class citizens were those who could in some way trace their ancestry to the tribes of the patriarchs, and hence to Abraham. Israelite faith always had a physical base, by affiliation, if not by direct descent. All the more reason then why family ties were sacred in Israel.

But the teaching of Jesus often brought a rupture in loyalties, and where blood and faith did not mix, there was no question in Jesus' mind which had precedence. The new Israel in Jesus is created by faith rather than by blood. There were blood relatives of Jesus who became his brothers through faith (for example, James, the "brother of the Lord," Gal 1:19; Acts 1:14). We also know this to be true for Mary, his mother. But it is faith, not the flesh, that gives entry to the kingdom. And it is faith, obedient faith, that brings one into the new family and makes one brother and sister and mother to Jesus.

16

Sower, Seed, and Soil

4:1-20

4 Again he began to teach beside the sea. And a very large crowd gathered about him, so that he got into a boat and sat in it on the sea; and the whole crowd was beside the sea on the land. ²And he taught them many things in parables, and in his teaching he said to them: ³"Listen! A sower went out to sow. ⁴And as he sowed, some seed fell along the path, and

the birds came and devoured it. ⁵Other seed fell on rocky ground, where it had not much soil, and immediately it sprang up, since it had no depth of soil; ⁶and when the sun rose it was scorched, and since it had no root it withered away. ⁷Other seed fell among thorns and the thorns grew up and choked it, and it yielded no grain. ⁸And other seeds fell into good soil and brought forth grain, growing up and increasing and yielding thirtyfold and sixtyfold and a hundredfold." ⁹And he said, "He who has ears to hear, let him hear."

¹⁰And when he was alone, those who were about him with the twelve asked him concerning the parables. ¹¹And he said to them, "To you has been given the secret of the kingdom of God, but for those outside everything is in parables; ¹²so that they may indeed see but not perceive, and may indeed hear but not understand; lest they should turn again, and be forgiven." ¹³And he said to them, "Do you not understand this parable? How then will you understand all the parables? ¹⁴The sower sows the word. ¹⁵And these are the ones along the path, where the word is sown; when they hear, Satan immediately comes and takes away the word which is sown in them. ¹⁶And these in like manner are the ones sown upon rocky ground, who, when they hear the word, immediately receive it with joy; ¹⁷and they have no root in themselves, but endure for a while; then, when tribulation or persecution arises on account of the word, immediately they fall away. ¹⁸And others are the ones sown among thorns; they are those who hear the word, ¹⁹but the cares of the world, and the delight in riches, and the desire for other things, enter in and choke the word, and it proves unfruitful. ²⁰But those that were sown upon the good soil are the ones who hear the word and accept it and bear fruit, thirtyfold and sixtyfold and a hundredfold."

BEGINNING WITH CHAPTER four, Mark gives us his first extended sample of the teaching of Jesus. Though there is less of

Jesus' teaching in Mark than in Luke or Matthew, it is no less important since it sets forth the real meaning of his miracles: The kingdom of God is at hand.

The setting is graphic. The seashore becomes a stadium and Peter's boat a pulpit, where, in Mark's colorful language, Jesus sits "on the sea." He teaches in "parables." We might almost say, "He taught them with stories," if by "story" we understand it in its broad meaning: proverb, fable, example, or riddle. Parables are stories that call for an interpretation. Some of the details of a story simply carry the story along while others have a symbolic meaning. When each of the details of a story is symbolic (as, for example, in the "Vine and the Branches" of Jn 15), we have an allegory in its pure form. When the story has just one point to illustrate it is called simply a parable. Many parables in our gospels are partly allegories, but it is always important to first determine the central point of the story.

What, then, is the central point of the parable of the sower? Up to this point, Jesus' ministry has been marked by phenomenal success on the one hand and by growing resistance on the other. The crowds have marveled at his teaching, demons have been driven out and many persons healed. But the officials have tried to block Jesus in every way and have accused him of being demon-possessed. Even his own family has tried to stop him. The disciples and the reader of the gospel might wonder why Jesus, the Son of God, does not have instant and universal success? How is it that the divine mission runs into delays, opposition, and varying degrees of success?

Jesus' answer is that he is like the Palestinian farmer, a man who might have been sowing on a nearby hillside as Jesus spoke. He sows by hand *before* plowing (unlike the modern farmer). He casts the grain everywhere; on the path that transients have worn across the field since harvest, on soil that is rocky, and even where there are weeds—since it will all be plowed under. The farmer knows that despite the varying conditions of the soil, his sowing will yield a rich harvest. So also with Jesus. He preaches now without screening his audiences, knowing that in the end the harvest will be great.

But a screening process takes place nonetheless, and Jesus addresses himself to it when he is alone with his disciples. Only to them is given the secret of the kingdom, for only they have authentic faith. The crowds, among whom are Jesus' enemies, do not have a committed faith. Only to the believers, therefore, is the secret revealed. It is not that God wishes to reveal the mystery to some and hide it from others. It is simply that his revelation is the occasion of faith for some and the occasion of disbelief for others. Disbelief, or lack of personal commitment, puts one on the path taken by the disbelieving generations of old, the scoffers of Isaiah's time who would not receive God's word. Today, as then, those who oppose the word or cannot give a decisive "yes" to it end up fulfilling in themselves the prophecy of Isaiah—they see without perceiving, hear without understanding.

In interpreting the parable for the disciples, Jesus first makes it clear how fundamental this parable is to understanding all his parables. (Matthew will also put it first in his chapter on the parables of the kingdom.) Then, while the parable itself stressed the confident and undaunted work of the sower (Jesus), the interpretation becomes allegorical and uses the various kinds of soil to symbolize the differing responses to the word. Some never really receive it in the first place. Others do and become disciples but fall away as soon as they have to pay the price of discipleship. Still others receive it, but they are not single-hearted. They are soon choked by worldly cares, love of riches, and desire for other things. Finally, there are the true disciples who not only hear the word but welcome it and bear fruit in messianic proportions—up to a hundredfold.

There is a lesson here, of course, about how disciples should live with the word they have already received. To be fruitful, they must cling to that word with perseverance and single-heartedness. But on a larger scale, the word is shown here to be both grace and judgment. It gives life, but it also brings to the surface the various tendencies in men's hearts. It has caused the separation of Jesus' disciples from the rest of the world, and even from those who could not take discipleship for long. But why should this be surprising? There is no harvest without sowing, no sowing without soil, and all soil varies in quality. Uneven results, the "waste" of the word on some, and the stark sifting of mankind have not stopped the divine Sower from sowing the word. Nor should this non-uniform outcome surprise the disciples or discourage them either from hearing the word or proclaiming it. Somewhere in the throwing there is good soil. The seed will find it and yield a prodigious harvest.

17

The Lamp and the Measure

4:21-25

[21]And he said to them, "Is a lamp brought in to be put under a bushel, or under a bed, and not on a stand? [22]For there is nothing hid, except to be made manifest; nor is anything secret, except to come to light. [23]If any man has ears to hear, let him hear." [24]And he said to them, "Take heed what you hear; the measure you give will be the measure you get, and still more will be given you. [25]For to him who has will more be given; and from him who has not, even what he has will be taken away."

HAVING PRESENTED THE parable of the sower, Mark now continues addressing the mystery of concealment and revelation. Why is the mystery of the kingdom—and the mystery of Jesus' identity—revealed to some and hidden from others?

Most English translations try to improve on Mark's rough Greek (as do Matthew and Luke) and read, "Is *a* lamp *brought in*?" or the equivalent (v. 21). But Mark's Greek says literally, "Does *the* lamp *come*?" Of course, this way of describing the entrance of a lamp could simply be the simpler Aramaic language bleeding through in clumsy Greek. But it seems more likely that Mark understands the lamp to be Jesus who *comes*. The verb *come*, in the gospel tradition and in Mark, has an important meaning for understanding Jesus. The Baptist hailed Jesus as the *coming* one (1:7). Jesus has *come* to preach the good news (1:38), to call sinners (2:17), to destroy Satan (1:24), to give his life as a ransom for many (10:45). This could be called the secret coming, in the sense that Jesus comes in lowliness, in service, and in signs. But there is another coming for which his disciples now wait: the coming in his Father's glory (8:38), the coming on the clouds of heaven (13:26; 14:62), the coming at the hour unknown (13:35-36).

Verse 22, which explains verse 21, implies that the lamp is indeed hidden for a while, but that concealment is neither the purpose of its coming nor its final status. Like a lamp that may be shielded by the hand until it has reached its resting place on the stand, so Jesus "comes" now in a partly concealed way but will be revealed in full light to all at the parousia, his glorious manifestation. Those who know how to read the signs in faith (those who have ears to hear, v. 23) see the light coming even now and await its full manifestation.

The same message is now reinforced in the parable of the measure, suggested perhaps by the bushel measure in the parable of the lamp. This parable is indeed a puzzle put by Jesus to make us think. "The measure you give" probably refers to our response to the teaching and person of Jesus now, in the obscurity of faith; this is suggested by the introductory words, "Take heed what you hear." If there is faith and receptivity now, there will be proportionate results later, far beyond measure, since we cannot even imagine the great things God has in store for us (see 1 Cor 2:9). That is why to him who possesses now what has been given him in obscurity (the seed of God's word) will be given much more. And from him who has refused the gift offered now, even what he has will be taken away.

The last statement invites us to pause and reflect on the way the word of God addresses our whole orientation toward life. It is, surely, a gift beyond our meriting, beyond our imagining, and beyond all our human power to produce. To receive it opens us to the radically new kingdom of God. At the same time, however, it does not mean that if we refuse the gift we can continue, humanly speaking, as well off as we were before hearing the word. For we must bear the effects of our own free choice, and to turn from the light and refuse "so great a salvation" (Heb 2:3), for whatever reason, can only result in impoverishing us, even in our human capacities to live and to love.

18

The Mystery of Growth
4:26-34

²⁶And he said, "The kingdom of God is as if a man should scatter seed upon the ground, ²⁷and should sleep and rise night and day, and the seed should sprout and grow, he knows not how. ²⁸The earth produces of itself, first the blade, then the ear, then the full grain in the ear. ²⁹But when the grain is ripe, at once he puts in the sickle, because the harvest has come."

³⁰And he said, "With what can we compare the kingdom of God, or what parable shall we use for it? ³¹It is like a grain of mustard seed, which, when sown upon the ground, is the smallest of all the seeds on earth; ³²yet when it is sown it grows up and becomes the greatest of all shrubs, and puts forth large branches, so that the birds of the air can make nests in its shade."

³³With many such parables he spoke the word to them, as they were able to hear it; ³⁴he did not speak to them without a parable, but privately to his own disciples he explained everything.

THIS SECTION CONTAINS two parables about growth (vv. 26-32) and a concluding statement about Jesus' habitual use of parables (vv. 33-34). A parable is a mystery to be decoded, and scholars disagree on exactly which of several possible points is the teaching of the first parable. Is it the patience of the farmer (and therefore of Jesus)? Or is it the mysterious self-growth of the seed? The latter is probably the better meaning. What a mystery is the growth of harvest from seed! The farmer sows, then waits. He waits, not because there is nothing else to do, but because something is already happening! He can't explain it, but he knows that's the way the harvest comes about.

It is likely that the harvest here stands for the judgment, the final act of God in establishing his reign; the language of sickle and ripe harvest echoes Joel 4:13, where it means God's judgment. The process has begun in the preaching of Jesus, and the word that has gone forth from him is God's word, which carries a marvelous fruitfulness in itself (see Is 55:10-11). Is Jesus restraining some of his Zealot-oriented disciples who would like to use violence to bring about the kingdom at once? This has been suggested, but we can't be sure Jesus meant to be that specific. What the parable does stress is that the sower, whether Jesus in his preaching or the disciples in theirs, should lay aside anxiety about results. Nor does God's sower need to use all-too-human means to accelerate the process. When harvest time comes the harvest will be there, because God's word, like seed, is endowed with life in itself.

While the parable of the sown grain focuses on the mysterious self-growth process, the parable of the mustard seed simply stresses the contrast of the end with the beginning. From the smallest of seeds, the largest of shrubs springs up. The nesting of birds in it may merely be a way of emphasizing its size, or it may be seen, in the light of Old Testament precedents, as an image for a mighty kingdom, even perhaps the incorporation of the Gentiles into God's family (see Ez 17:23; 31:5-6; Dn 4:7-21).

In the case of both parables we are confronted with an understanding of the *word* which is foreign to our usual perception of it. The fact that only our written words will hold up in court has led our Western culture to view the spoken word like the wind that comes and goes but is without substance. Not so more primitive cultures, which often consider the demand to put an agreement in writing an insult to integrity. And certainly the Bible considers that when a person utters a word his whole being is involved. More than that, a persons' word can actually create the future, either in blessing or in curse—and in either case the word once spoken takes on an independent existence. When Isaac, even though in error, gave his paternal blessing to Jacob instead of to Esau, he could not recall the blessing. The best he could do was to send out a second blessing to neutralize somewhat the effects of the one given to Jacob (Gn 27). This power of words to work long after they have been spoken also explains why evil and malicious speech is so condemned in the Bible.

If such power is found when man speaks, how much more when God speaks! His word is like fire, like a hammer shattering rock (Jer 23:29); it is keener than a two-edged sword (Heb 4:12); it is like rain that brings the harvest (Is 55:10-11); it creates (Gn 1); it is life for mankind (Dt 8:3). Jesus tells us that it is like seed in its power and independence. Anyone who has seen Johnson grass break through pavement knows the power of a tiny seed—and its independence.

The overriding impression we get, then, from the parables of this chapter is one of immense confidence in the power of God's word to achieve the end for which it was sent. There may indeed be obstacles, but God's word will be fruitful nonetheless. That word, in the context here, is Jesus' preaching of the kingdom. A harvest is in preparation. Jesus has confidently sown the seed.

If he has spoken in parables—that is, in enigmatic speech—it has been an act of mercy as well as judgment. Too much light at once might blind those who have at least a minimum of good will. The full meaning can be entrusted only to disciples—to those who are willing to commit their lives to Jesus. Understanding for the disciple does not precede but follows upon commitment.

Lord of Wind and Sea

4:35-41

³⁵On that day, when evening had come, he said to them, "Let us go across to the other side." ³⁶And leaving the crowd, they took him with them, just as he was, in the boat. And other boats were with him. ³⁷And a great storm of wind arose, and the waves beat into the boat, so that the boat was already filling. ³⁸But he was in the stern, asleep on the cushion; and they woke him and said to him, "Teacher, do you not care if we perish?" ³⁹And he awoke and rebuked the wind, and said to the sea, "Peace! Be still!" And the wind ceased, and there was a great calm. ⁴⁰He said to them, "Why are you afraid? Have you no faith?" ⁴¹And they were filled with awe, and said to one another, "Who then is this, that even wind and sea obey him?"

THE STORY OF Jesus' encounter with the chaotic powers of nature can be studied at the various levels of its development: in the actual life of Jesus, in the catechetical and symbolic importance this story soon took on in the life of the early community, and, finally, in the teaching Mark wishes to convey through it.

There are many details in the story that sound like a vivid and even personal reminiscence from the life of Jesus: taking him "as he was," the other boats (not essential to the story), the pillow, the surprisingly heavy sleep of Jesus, the tone of rebuke in the disciples' cry for help. The early community considered the boat a symbol of the church and the story a lesson in discipleship; this element is probably already at work in our present text. Finally, Mark himself is interested in raising the question of who Jesus is. The reader already knows that the

Jesus asleep in the boat is the Messiah and Son of God (1:1), but the disciples have not yet come to that realization. Thus the reader is led, through the disciples' fear, ignorance, and still deficient faith, to probe the mystery of this man who can calm the sea with a word.

The sun has already slipped behind the Galilean hills forming the west side of the gigantic basin which is the Sea of Galilee. The lengthening shadows announce nightfall. Jesus has finished his teaching for the day. He suggests going to the eastern shore, a distance of six or seven miles. We are not told why Jesus suggests this, though we know, from reading ahead, that an important ministry awaits him at the other side. It was not, apparently, just to give the disciples an opportunity to do some night fishing, though such was common practice when the brisk afternoon breeze had abated. A windstorm at night would be unusual and dangerous but not inconceivable in the saucer-like sea, proverbially the stage of rapid changes of wind and weather.

This is just what happens. In a matter of minutes the waves are filling the boat. Jesus is asleep. This detail, the only instance of his sleeping recorded in the gospels, is a brilliant commentary on Jesus' humanness and the hiddenness of his divine identity, a favorite theme in Mark. His disciples have enough faith to wake him, but they address him as teacher, and there is a tone of rebuke in their question: "Don't you care?"

Mark describes Jesus' action in exactly the same language he uses to describe the exorcisms. Jesus *rebukes* the wind, just as he did the demons (1:25; 3:12; 9:25), and tells the sea, as he would a person, "Peace, be still" (cf. 1:25; 4:39). To understand the imagery here, it will be helpful to recall that the wind and the sea are ancient biblical symbols for chaos. Whether this be the primeval chaos of creation (Gn 1:1), the political chaos of nations in tumult (Ps 65:8), the storm that sailors face (Ps 107:23-30), or simply overwhelming personal distress (Ps 34:5-6), the Lord of Israel is master of this chaotic wind and sea (Prv 30:4; Jb 28:25; Am 4:13). The chief historical manifestation of this is in the Exodus, where the waters saw God and fled (Ps

77:17-20; 114:3-5). What we have here, then, is a similar mastery over the cosmic forces, especially when their fury is of demonic proportions. Jesus' conquest of the demons and of the storm are of one piece. The terrifying cosmic powers yield before the Lord of wholeness and cosmic order.

It is not clear exactly where the lesson about faith lies. Did the disciples show lack of faith by waking Jesus? Or did they awaken him only with a rebuke and not a specific request to calm the sea, thus betraying their lack of understanding of his power? Their final comment would suggest the latter interpretation, and it is certainly Mark's point: Who is he? The reader will supply the answer: "Obviously, the Son of God!"

When the community or the individual goes through a storm and fears sinking, the disciple's faith is challenged to believe not only that Jesus is present and is caring for his own, but that he is also *Lord* of the chaos; his limitless power can meet and redeem the most terrifying disaster.

20

Jesus Frees and Restores

5:1-20

5 They came to the other side of the sea, to the country of the Gerasenes. ²And when he had come out of the boat, there met him out of the tombs a man with an unclean spirit, ³who lived among the tombs; and no one could bind him any more, even with a chain; ⁴for he had often been bound with fetters and chains, but the chains he wrenched apart, and the fetters he broke in pieces; and no one had the strength to subdue him. ⁵Night and day among the tombs and on the mountains he was always crying out, and bruising

himself with stones. [6]And when he saw Jesus from afar, he ran and worshiped him; [7]and crying out with a loud voice, he said, "What have you to do with me, Jesus, Son of the Most High God? I adjure you by God, do not torment me." [8]For he had said to him, "Come out of the man, you unclean spirit!" [9]And Jesus asked him, "What is your name?" He replied, "My name is Legion; for we are many." [10]And he begged him eagerly not to send them out of the country. [11]Now a great herd of swine was feeding there on the hillside; [12]and they begged him, "Send us to the swine, let us enter them." [13]So he gave them leave. And the unclean spirits came out, and entered the swine; and the herd, numbering about two thousand, rushed down the steep bank into the sea, and were drowned in the sea.

[14]The herdsmen fled, and told it in the city and in the country. And people came to see what it was that had happened. [15]And they came to Jesus, and saw the demoniac sitting there, clothed and in his right mind, the man who had had the legion; and they were afraid. [16]And those who had seen it told what had happened to the demoniac and to the swine. [17]And they began to beg Jesus to depart from their neighborhood. [18]And as he was getting into the boat, the man who had been possessed with demons begged him that he might be with him. [19]But he refused, and said to him, "Go home to your friends, and tell them how much the Lord has done for you, and how he has had mercy on you." [20]And he went away and began to proclaim in the Decapolis how much Jesus had done for him; and all men marveled.

JESUS AND HIS disciples arrive on the eastern bank of the Sea of Galilee, probably near modern Kersa. To the south of Kersa lies a steep slope and a little further south cavern tombs have been found. It is helpful to think of the demoniac's condition as the negative of Mark's photograph of redemption. Jesus' action is a teaching on what a saving encounter with him achieves. The possessed man is experiencing a living death—his home is among the tombs. He is self-destructive, suicidal, violent. The fears of his violence had led his townspeople to attempt chaining him, but his superhuman energy snapped the chains, indicating not his freedom but his slavery to an even greater power—an "unclean spirit."

He is alienated not only from his own sanity but from human community. He is driven by a force like that of an army. A Roman legion at this time comprised 6000 footsoldiers and 120 calvary. This name suggests the tremendous power of the demons' presence, their lack of identifiable personality (all soldiers dress and look alike), and the multiple directions in which the man is compulsively driven, as in schizophrenia. He is neither free nor whole.

His actions as Jesus approaches are typically contradictory. He runs toward Jesus and falls down in worship. But at the same time he wants to ward off Jesus by naming him. "The Most High God" was a title often used by or in connection with Gentiles for the supreme God (Gn 14:18; Nm 24:16; Is 14:14; Dn 3:93). To name a divine power was, in popular thought, to have control over it. Jesus, however, forces the demons to reveal their own name, Legion. Aware of Jesus' superior power, they offer a compromise: Instead of tormenting us (compare "destroy" in 1:24) or sending us out of the country, let us go into the swine.

It is important to note that this alternative was not suggested by Jesus, only allowed by him. Scholars have long debated why he allows this destruction of a herd of two thousand swine. Jesus' own Jewish disciples probably would have had no scruple about it and would even applaud this spectacular riddance, in pagan territory, of what they held to be unclean animals. However, the destruction of the swine brings into the open what would ultimately have happened to the man the demons were possessing. Perhaps, too, through Jesus' allowing the demons a place to go, Mark intends to show his ultimate conquest over the demonic kingdom is yet to come—on the cross!

There may, however, be still another lesson. Note how the townspeople show more concern for their pigs than they do for their restored brother. How their values contrast with those of Jesus! Might it be that their social structure, like many impersonal structures of our modern culture, was so focused on material welfare that it created the very environment for the depersonalization of a member of their community? Are your pigs more important to you than your brother?

The man is redeemed. He sits fully clothed (a detail Mark uses to describe the witness of the resurrection in 16:5, just as nakedness and flight mark the hour of unredeemed weakness, 14:50-51). He is "in his right mind." And he now wants to follow Jesus as a disciple (to be "with him" has this meaning in Mark 3:14). But there is an element of the man's healing which has yet to be completed: his reintegration into his family and community, for they have yet to accept his redemption! So Jesus sends the restored man to his own people as a missionary and witness. Jesus may have been the occasion of the loss of their swine, but he will not take from them the brother they have not yet welcomed back—the brother who will give them a chance, if they are willing to change, to see the whole event as the good news of God's kingdom.

The story then is more than just another victory of Jesus over powers hostile to God. It is a lesson in what deliverance and healing is all about, not just for the individual but for the community.

21

Jesus Conquers Even Death

5:21-43

[21]And when Jesus had crossed again in the boat to the other side, a great crowd gathered about him; and he was beside the sea. [22]Then came one of the rulers of the synagogue, Jairus by name; and seeing him, he fell at his feet, [23]and besought him, saying, "My little daughter is at the point of death. Come and lay your hands on her, so that she may be made well, and live." [24]And he went with him.

And a great crowd followed him and thronged about him. [25]And there was a woman who had had a flow of blood for twelve years, [26]and who had suffered much under many physicians, and had spent all that she had, and was no better but rather grew worse. [27]She had heard the reports about Jesus, and came up behind him in the crowd and touched his garment. [28]For she said, "If I touch even his garments, I shall be made well." [29]And immediately the hemorrhage ceased; and she felt in her body that she was healed of her disease. [30]And Jesus, perceiving in himself that power had gone forth from him, immediately turned about in the crowd, and said, "Who touched my garments?" [31]And his disciples said to him, "You see the crowd pressing around you, and yet you say, 'Who touched me?'" [32]And he looked around to see who had done it. [33]But the woman, knowing what had been done to her, came in fear and trembling and fell down before him, and told him the whole truth. [34]And he said to her, "Daughter, your faith has made you well; go in peace, and be healed of your disease."

[35]While he was still speaking, there came from the

ruler's house some who said, "Your daughter is dead. Why trouble the Teacher any further?" [36]But ignoring what they said, Jesus said to the ruler of the synagogue, "Do not fear, only believe." [37]And he allowed no one to follow him except Peter and James and John the brother of James. [38]When they came to the house of the ruler of the synagogue, he saw a tumult, and people weeping and wailing loudly. [39]And when he had entered, he said to them, "Why do you make a tumult and weep? The child is not dead but sleeping." [40]And they laughed at him. But he put them all outside, and took the child's father and mother and those who were with him, and went in where the child was. [41]Taking her by the hand he said to her, "Talitha cumi"; which means, "Little girl, I say to you, arise." [42]And immediately the girl got up and walked; for she was twelve years old. And immediately they were overcome with amazement. [43]And he strictly charged them that no one should know this, and told them to give her something to eat.

THIS IS THE only place in the gospels where one miracle story is interrupted by another. Doubtless this kind of surprising sequence happened more than once in Jesus' busy ministry of healing. For Mark, however, the unit here is important as a lesson about faith in the power of Jesus.

Jairus, a religious man, held one of the most important positions in town. As a ruler of the synagogue he was responsible for its maintenance and the order of service. His twelve-year-old daughter was at the point of death. In his distress during her illness he had perhaps sought for Jesus, only to learn he was out of town. Then when word came that the wonder-worker had just disembarked, Jairus ran through the crowd that was already gathered and threw himself at Jesus' feet: "Come, lay your hands on her, that she may get well *and live*." "And live" is obviously superfluous, but it carries the vehement love and hope Jairus has for his daughter. It also focuses our attention on what will be the surprise and the lesson of the whole story.

Jairus is doubtless relieved and grateful that Jesus agrees to come. He begins "running interference" for him through the jostling crowds, as one would hastily usher a doctor to the scene of an accident.

But suddenly Jesus is no longer following. Looking back, Jairus sees a disturbance around Jesus, who himself has stopped and turned around. A woman who has been hemorrhaging for twelve years (and in Mark's elaborate description has suffered much from many physicians, only to get worse) has touched Jesus' garment and been cured instantly. She had faith, but she also knew that in her state the law declared her unclean. As such she would ritually contaminate anyone who touched her. This could be compromising for Jesus—but why would he need to know, if she just touched his garments in the midst of the crowd? (Some scholars think her approach is tinged with magical beliefs, but it seems more likely that the problem of ritual defilement is the real issue.) Jesus, at any rate, knows that "power has gone out from him." Mark sees Jesus as a living dynamo, which, when contacted by faith, inevitably releases power. The woman senses at once that she is healed. Jesus does not allow her to escape anonymously in the crowd but cries out, "Who touched my garments?" The woman comes forward and publicly confesses her action and her gratitude to Jesus. Jesus *then* pronounces the word of healing. This account carries an important teaching: First, healing is a personal encounter with Jesus. It is not a magical or mechanical event, though physical touch may be involved. The healed person must meet Jesus, even if the meeting takes place *after* the healing. Second, a public confession of Jesus is part of the healing process. Others may thus come to faith through this woman's witness. Finally, even though the physical event of her healing has taken place already, Jesus' *word* of healing completes the action. He further personalizes it, and teaches that her touch would have been meaningless without faith.

For Jairus, the interruption has been doubly critical. He has witnessed Jesus' power to heal, but the delay has cost the life of his daughter. Those who bring news of the girl's death suggest that Jesus come no farther. Jesus, however, ignores the suggestion and continues with Jairus, promising nothing, challenging him to believe. Twelve years of bleeding had stopped—but so had twelve years of life! Even now, in the face of death, could Jairus continue to believe? Could he afford not to? He had asked Jesus, after all, that his daughter *live*.

To Jesus the girl is only asleep, but the evidence and the witnesses say she is dead. "Sleep" here is intended by Mark and perhaps by Jesus as faith's way of understanding death in the light of the promised resurrection (see 1 Thes 5:10 and Jn 11:11-13). It is as easy for Jesus to raise from the dead as it is for us to arouse someone from sleep. Jesus raises the girl to life, in a way unimagined by Jairus in his first faith request that she live (v. 23).

Only her parents and the three disciples witness the secret. For though the scoffers may ultimately see its effects, they cannot see the miracle itself. Only a believing community discerns the real miracle—that this is a raising from death (as Luke surely understands, Lk 8:55), and not just an awakening from a sleep-like coma. Such, at least, seems to be the meaning of Jesus' curious and otherwise impossible command to keep the miracle a secret.

The story ends on a very human note as Jesus reminds the excited parents that the child could benefit by something to eat.

22

Rejection at Home

6:1-6

6 He went away from there and came to his own country; and his disciples followed him. [2]And on the sabbath he began to teach in the synagogue; and many who heard him were astonished, saying, "Where did this man get all this? What is the wisdom given to him? What mighty works are wrought by his hands! [3]Is not this the carpenter, the son of Mary and brother of James and Joses and Judas and Simon, and are not his sisters here with us?" And they took offense at him. [4]And Jesus said to them, "A prophet is not without honor, except in his own country, and among his own kin, and in his own house." [5]And he could do no mighty work there, except that he laid his hands upon a few sick people and healed them. [6]And he marveled because of their unbelief.

AFTER THE AMAZING double-miracle in the seashore town, Jesus works his way southwestward through the Galilean hills to "his own country," which we may understand to be Nazareth. In noting that the disciples follow him, Mark prepares us not only for their mission (6:7) but also their rejection (6:11), since their experience will follow the pattern of their master.

Mark has telescoped here what may in fact have been a longer ministry with a more complex development. Jesus begins to teach in the synagogue. Whether by "many" Mark means a large portion of the congregation or a generalizing "all" is not clear. Nor is it clear how their apparently positive reaction in verse 2 is related to his listeners taking offense at him in verse 3. From verse 5 we can assume that the astonishing mighty works are ones he has done elsewhere (as Luke seems to understand in his version, Lk 4:23). The townsfolk are curious, then, and are seeking signs for their own sake, not as a healing encounter of faith which effects conversion. With this attitude it is easy to see how they could go on to imply that the signs Jesus did elsewhere were not authentic, or at least had no indication of a divine origin. Jesus, after, was not a rabbi, and his origins were the humblest. He was a well-known carpenter of the village. While the trade may have been respectable enough in the Nazareth of Jesus' day, by the second century, Celsus, a great antagonist of Christianity, sneered at the fact that its founder was nothing but a carpenter by trade. Indeed Christianity ever since has had to deal with the fact that the man it acknowledges to be Lord and Son of God came out of a workshop rather than a university.

Some scholars think "son of Mary" on the lips of the townspeople was intended as a slur, indicating some knowledge of the unusual character of Jesus' conception, which they take to be illegitimate. The church that preserved this gospel and believed in the virgin birth would have no difficulty in understanding "son of Mary" as an allusion to the mysterious divine conception. However, the more probable view is that this is neither a reference to illegitimacy nor to the virgin birth. While it is true that officially a man would be referred to as the son of his father, even after his father's death, Luke 7:12 shows that this was not always the case in popular description, for there the young man is "the only son of his mother who was a widow." If Joseph has in fact died (highly plausible since unlike Mary he makes no appearance in any of the gospels after Jesus' baptism), then "son of Mary," like the reference to the brothers and sisters, refers simply to the living parent well known in the village.

The "brothers and sisters" mentioned here can mean, as in many primitive cultures today, members of the extended family and not necessarily siblings of the first degree (see Gn 24:48 and 29:12). "Brother" in Mark 6:17-18 means "step-brother." Hence this text offers no linguistic evidence against the faith of many Christians in the perpetual virginity of Mary.

The obstacle to faith in the Nazareth community, then, simply is the scandal of Jesus' ordinariness. It is not unlike the tendency today to think the only speaker worth listening to is one brought from elsewhere by jet. There is a universal tendency to think that the great works of God always occur elsewhere. Underlying this is a lack of faith that they could happen here, which may even lead one to question or deny that they indeed happened elsewhere. Ironically, this is precisely what prevents God from acting. Jesus first quotes a proverb about a prophet being received everywhere but among his own people. Then he finds his power to work miracles limited, not in itself, but by the lack of faith of the community. Mark does allow that there was a remnant of faith-filled people who benefited by Jesus' ministry, but the emphasis is on the wave of disbelief he encountered. Jesus "marveled." This single word, the only place Mark uses it of him, tells us much about Jesus' humanness. He could be surprised! Though he was Son of God (1:1; 15:39), his reaction was as human as ours when confronted by the unexpected.

The rejection by his townfolk not only echoes the previous hostility Jesus has experienced (3:6, 20-35) but also prepares us for the mission of the disciples which immediately follows (6:6-13). Thus it is a distant preparation for the passion and death of Jesus, which opened the way to the mission of the disciples to every creature (see 16:15).

23

Jesus Sends the Twelve

6:6-13

⁶And he went about among the villages teaching.

⁷And he called to him the twelve, and began to send them out two by two, and gave them authority over the unclean spirits. ⁸He charged them to take nothing for their journey except a staff; no bread, no bag, no money in their belts; ⁹but to wear sandals and not put on two tunics. ¹⁰And he said to them, "Where you enter a house, stay there until you leave the place. ¹¹And if any place will not receive you and they refuse to hear you, when you leave, shake off the dust that is on your feet for a testimony against them." ¹²So they went out and preached that men should repent. ¹³And they cast out many demons, and anointed with oil many that were sick and healed them.

HAVING BEEN REJECTED in his home village, Jesus tours elsewhere, thus setting a pattern which the early church would later follow (Acts 8:4). His effectiveness is apparently greater, and he wishes to respond to the needs of people in villages he cannot reach by his personal presence. In sending the Twelve, Jesus shows that his mission transcends his own human limitations—collaborators will carry on his work. He has carefully prepared for this by calling the fishing brothers (1:16-20), then Levi (2:14), then by selecting the Twelve (3:13-19), instructing them more privately than the crowds (4:11, 34) and modeling for them a ministry of deliverance and healing (chapter 5).

Sending them out in twos is a provision for mutual support, surely, as well as a caution against individualism. Jesus preferred that his disciples exercise a team ministry! But more important for the Jewish mind of the day, two witnesses were considered necessary to establish the truth of any claim (Nm

35:30; Dt 17:6; 19:15). This will be important whether their witness is accepted or rejected. If the claim of the apostles is accepted, they witness to God in favor of those who receive it; if rejected, they consign the hearers to God's judgment.

Jesus gives them *exousia*, a Greek word meaning both power and authorization. In his *exousia*, Jesus is personally present to each of the six teams he sends out. They will continue his own conquest of Satan's kingdom.

They are cautioned, however, to depend totally on Jesus' *exousia* and not on human resources. Their dependence on God is mirrored by a dependence on the hospitality of those to whom they go—a magnificent way of allowing the receiver the dignity of having something to give.

We need not get distracted by discussions about whether staff and sandals are permitted. Mark allows them, Matthew does not, and Luke prohibits sandals while saying nothing about staff. The point of the description in each case is poverty of means and vulnerability to God's providence and men's hospitality. This is true even of the command to take only one tunic. A second tunic would provide covering for sleeping outdoors in the night chill. Renouncing this security means relying on others for shelter.

Nor are they to leave one host to accept better accomodations from another. It is not the accommodations that are important to the mission but the heart of the receiver who shares whatever means he has.

The early church soon found that such hospitality could be abused by later missionaries who were perhaps not as well motivated as the Twelve. The first century *Didache* ("Teaching of the Apostles") says that a missionary visit should not last more than two days. Even Paul at times worked to support himself, lest his motives be misread.

When a town rejected the evangelists, they were to shake the dust from their feet as a testimony against it. Pious Jews who passed through pagan territory would often do this as a measure of avoiding their own defilement by the pagan environment. Here, however, it is a prophetic action intended as a final warning to the unrepentant: The only alternative to the mercy of God is the judgment of God!

The disciples proclaim the message of repentance, cast out demons, and heal the sick, anointing them with oil. Oil was a common remedy for the sick or wounded (see Lk 10:34), and in the later church it became a visible way of applying to the believer the power of Jesus, the anointed one (*Christos*).

The mission recorded here is, of course, a temporary one during the public ministry of Jesus. Nevertheless, it prepares and models the future mission given to the disciples by the risen Lord.

24

A Slain Prophet Lives On

6:14-29

[14]King Herod heard of it; for Jesus' name had become known. Some said, "John the baptizer has been raised from the dead; that is why these powers are at work in him." [15]But others said, "It is Elijah." And others said, "It is a prophet, like one of the prophets of old." [16]But when Herod heard of it he said, "John, whom I beheaded, has been raised." [17]For Herod had sent and seized John, and bound him in prison for the sake of Herodias, his brother Philip's wife; because he had married her. [18]For John said to Herod, "It is not lawful for you to have your brother's wife." [19]And Herodias had a grudge against him, and wanted to kill him. But she could not, [20]for Herod feared John, knowing that he was a righteous and holy man, and kept him safe. When he heard him, he was much perplexed; and yet he heard him gladly. [21]But an opportunity came when Herod on his birthday gave a banquet for his courtiers

and officers and the leading men of Galilee. [22]For when Herodias' daughter came in and danced, she pleased Herod and his guests; and the king said to the girl, "Ask me for whatever you wish, and I will grant it." [23]And he vowed to her, "Whatever you ask me, I will give you, even half of my kingdom." [24]And she went out, and said to her mother, "What shall I ask?" And she said, "The head of John the baptizer." [25]And she came in immediately with haste to the king, and asked, saying, "I want you to give me at once the head of John the Baptist on a platter." [26]And the king was exceedingly sorry; but because of his oaths and his guests he did not want to break his word to her. [27]And immediately the king sent a soldier of the guard and gave orders to bring his head. He went and beheaded him in the prison, [28]and brought his head on a platter, and gave it to the girl; and the girl gave it to her mother. [29]When his disciples heard of it, they came and took his body, and laid it in a tomb.

JESUS' MINISTRY HAS been effective and, with the sending out of the Twelve, even more widespread. People who have known of John the Baptist and Jesus only by hearsay now begin to talk about the relation of the two, since Jesus' ministry has followed closely upon John's. John was known as a holy man and a preacher of God's expectations, but not as a worker of signs. The fact that Jesus' ministry, marked by signs, began after John's imprisonment and eventual execution by Herod suggests to some that John has been raised from the dead—for the signs Jesus performs are so amazing (like raising the dead!) that they can scarcely be explained as the work of an ordinary mortal. They are signs of the world to come given already now, signs of one risen from the dead. So they conclude that Jesus must be John risen from the dead.

Others, agreeing that Jesus' signs are works of a man from the other world, conclude that Jesus is Elijah who was taken into heavenly glory (2 Kgs 2:11) and was to return before the great and terrible day of the Lord (Mal 3:23-24). John, after all, foretold just such a *coming* one (1:7), so it is understandable that some think of Jesus as Elijah come back.

In either case, people are not thinking of a royal messiah but of a wonder-working prophet. The last group likewise identifies Jesus as a prophet, but not as one returned to earth. They simply identify him as one *"like* the prophets of old." This would have been surprising enough, since the voice of prophecy had been virtually dead in Israel for the last two hundred years.

Herod, however, agrees with the first group, and with all the more certainty since it was he who beheaded John. John's resurrection would herald the judgment of God, at least upon Herod. This Herod is not the Herod of Jesus' childhood but Herod Antipas, who ruled Galilee and Perea from 4 B.C. to 39 A.D. Though he modeled his court on that of the emperor and may have been known popularly as "king," it was actually his seeking this title (on Herodias' prompting!) that led to his disgrace and exile by Rome in 39 A.D.

Mark proceeds to give us a flashback on the circumstances of John's death. A preacher of reform, John had let no one escape the finger of his judgment, not even the royal court. When Herod Antipas married his brother's wife, Herodias, John branded the union as adultery and scandal. To allow John to continue this public accusation was likely to foster unrest among the people, and Antipas was having enough trouble keeping the powerful neighboring Nabataean kingdom at bay to permit any trouble at home. Imprisoning John was, however, also an act of protective custody, for Herodias would have silenced him by immediate execution. Antipas was one of those tragic, indecisive figures who can admire a holy man, listen to his words at length, and even feel remorse, but cannot make the kind of about-face that real conversion requires. He is, to the very end, the real prisoner of the story. Herodias waits for the opportunity to use his power for her own purposes.

On his birthday, Antipas is entertaining his lords, military leaders, and courtiers—all terms which fit the court of a petty monarch trying to imitate the emperor. The Jewish historian

Josephus tells us that the name of Herodias' daughter was Salome. Well coached by her mother, she performs a sensuous dance, all the more pleasing to Herod and his guests as it is performed by the princess. In the midst of the applause, Antipas, in a moment of reveling generosity, offers to give Salome anything she wants. "Half my kingdom" was a proverbial expression of magnanimity (1 Kgs 13:8; Est 5:3, 6; Lk 19:8). He confirms the offer by oath. Salome consults her mother (an indication she was yet unmarried) and on returning asks for the head of John the Baptist, adding the gruesome detail that it be presented on a platter. Herod is distressed, but he is so imprisoned by the opinion of his guests that he yields to the request. John is beheaded and the macabre ritual is performed.

Mark's account is more than just a flashback to explain why Jesus was viewed by many, including Antipas, as John risen from the dead. It is yet another forecast of Jesus' fate. There exist many parallels between the passion of John and that of Jesus: a prophetic witness arouses the hatred of those who refuse to repent, the prophet is arrested, an official approved by Rome is sympathetic toward him, even holding him to be a righteous man; but in weakness the official finally grants the execution, and disciples come and lay the body in a tomb.

In 9:9-13 the parallel between Jesus and John in their suffering is made more explicit. John the Baptist suffered at the hands of a wicked woman and a weak king as had Elijah (1 Kgs 19). Jesus will be exalted in his resurrection from the dead, but first he must pay the price of his prophetic vocation just as John the Baptist did.

25

Bread in the Wilderness

6:30-44

[30]The apostles returned to Jesus, and told him all that they had done and taught. [31]And he said to them, "Come away by yourselves to a lonely place, and rest a while." For many were coming and going, and they had no leisure even to eat. [32]And they went away in the boat to a lonely place by themselves. [33]Now many saw them going, and knew them, and they ran there on foot from all the towns, and got there ahead of them. [34]As he landed he saw a great throng, and he had compassion on them, because they were like sheep without a shepherd; and he began to teach them many things. [35]And when it grew late, his disciples came to him and said, "This is a lonely place, and the hour is now late; [36]send them away, to go into the country and villages round about and buy themselves something to eat." [37]But he answered them, "You give them something to eat." And they said to him, "Shall we go and buy two hundred denarii worth of bread, and give it to them to eat? [38]And he said to them, "How many loaves have you? Go and see." And when they had found out, they said, "Five, and two fish." [39]Then he commanded them all to sit down by companies upon the green grass. [40]So they sat down in groups, by hundreds and by fifties. [41]And taking the five loaves and the two fish he looked up to heaven, and blessed, and broke the loaves, and gave them to the disciples to set before the people; and he divided the two fish among them all. [42]And they all ate and were satisfied. [43]And they took up twelve baskets full of broken pieces and of the fish. [44]And those who ate the loaves were five thousand men.

MARK HAS JUST related the story of Herod and John the Baptist, introduced by Herod's conviction that the signs now worked by Jesus and his company mean John has been raised from the dead. Herod is mistaken, of course, but in Mark's view he is right in seeing the healing ministry as the intrusion of the world to come into the present. The day will come when the signs worked by the disciples will be signs that *Jesus* is risen from the dead.

The apostles (as Mark calls them because they were "sent") return from their mission with an enthusiastic report. After listening to it, Jesus wants to go away to a wilderness place where they may rest and eat in peace. The ensuing event, however, is another of those surprises that reveal God's glory. The account of this event must be read at two levels: the simple event, and the deeper symbolism Mark sees in it.

A vast crowd gathers unexpectedly in the wilderness to share the disciples' rest and food. Anyone who has sought some peace and quiet and has been deprived of it can sympathize with the disciples as well as be impressed by Jesus' willingness to change his plans. But what is really taking place is a messianic fulfillment of the Old Testament.

As the Lord had once led his people through the desert to their resting place (Dt 3:20; 12:9-10; Jos 21:44; Ps 95:7-11), he promised to do so again (Jer 31:2; Is 63:14), and so "rest" became a symbol of the messianic kingdom (see Heb 3-4). When Moses asked the Lord for a successor, lest his people in the desert be "like sheep without a shepherd" (Mk 6:34), the Lord gave him Joshua (translated into Greek as "Jesus"). Ezekiel had prophesied another gift of a shepherd (Ez 34:23-24). In the desert the people of God had been divided into "hundreds and fifties" (Ex 18:21), and in Jesus' time members of the Dead Sea monastery of Qumran believed that this was the way the true Israel would be grouped in the desert in the final days. Finally, Psalm 23 had spoken of the Lord as the true shepherd leading his sheep to rest in green pastures and feeding them.

Mark sees all of this fulfilled in the wonderful feeding of the crowds in the wilderness. It is not simply a miracle. There is, of course, a marvelous lesson presented to the disciples about inadequate means becoming, in Jesus' hands, more than enough. But Jesus does not make a show of the multiplication either. He makes no attempt to provide more than a peasant's fare (in contrast to the sumptuous revelry in Herod's palace). Yet is is fully satisfying for everyone, as was the manna, of which this is now the fulfillment. Even the detail about the green grass is more than a graphic personal reminiscence. In the final times the wilderness was to become lush (Is 41:18-20; 5:3); the Lord-Shepherd has here, indeed, given his people rest in green pastures (Ps 23:2).

Thus we can say that Mark sees in the crowds, gathered with the disciples in the wilderness, the people of the new Exodus. Of course, the moment is only passing; there is no covenant formed here, no lasting relationship established between Jesus and the people. Neither is the meal yet the banquet of rich food and choice wine promised for the kingdom (Is 25:6). But the event does fulfill what God began in the desert with the people of old, and in turn forecasts the covenant meal Jesus will one day celebrate with his disciples (Mk 14:22-25).

Unfortunately, the disciples, who are the immediate witnesses of the miracle, do not grasp what it means (6:52). This lack of understanding will play an important role in the unfolding of the rest of the gospel. But the reader can understand, with Mark's help, that God's history and God's last word to his people are being acted out. In this "unplanned" interruption of a vacation, the Lord fulfilled what he had begun centuries earlier when he fed and gave rest to a people drawn to him in the desert.

26

Encounter at Sea

6:45-52

[45]Immediately he made his disciples get into the boat and go before him to the other side, to Bethsaida, while he dismissed the crowd. [46]And after he had taken leave of them, he went into the hills to pray. [47]And when evening came, the boat was out on the sea, and he was alone on the land. [48]And he saw that they were distressed in rowing, for the wind was against them. And about the fourth watch of the night he came to them, walking on the sea. He meant to pass by them, [49]but when they saw him walking on the sea they thought it was a ghost, and cried out; [50]for they all saw him, and were terrified. But immediately he spoke to them and said, "Take heart, it is I; have no fear." [51]And he got into the boat with them and the wind ceased. And they were utterly astounded. [52]for they did not understand about the loaves, but their hearts were hardened.

WE CAN DETECT a note of haste in Jesus' sending his disciples away and dismissing the crowd. Only in John's gospel are we told the reason: the crowd wanted to make Jesus king (Jn 6:14-15). Such a leap from identifying Jesus as a prophet to seeing him as the potential leader of a revolt would be completely in keeping with what we know of Galilee in this period. It was a hotbed of resistance to Rome.

But Jesus has other plans. As on an earlier day of highly successful ministry (1:35), he retires to commune with the Father and to root his entire ministry in his will. From the mountain it would not have been impossible, on a moonlit night, to follow a boat's progress with the naked eye. Jesus' view of the disciples, therefore, need not have been clairvoyance. The point in any case is that even at a distance Jesus knows his disciples' distress. At about three o'clock in the morning he comes to them, walking on the sea. It is not a magical show but rather a manifestation of Jesus' care for his disciples.

Why then does the text say, "He meant to pass by them"? Is this narrated simply from the viewpoint of the disciples who thought he was going to pass them by? Or does it mean that Jesus was going to pass *their way*—i.e., come directly toward them? Either explanation is a possible reading of the Greek, but a third may have even more weight. Readers familiar with the Old Testament will recognize a parallel here with the Lord's "passing by" Moses to give him a glimpse of his glory (Ex 33:19, 22). Later the Lord did the same for Elijah (1 Kgs 19:11). Mark, then, would be understanding the event as a theophany, a revelation of God himself in Jesus and a way of telling the disciples who Jesus really is. That the Lord might pass by without being recognized has a further foundation in a passage in Job, which some scholars believe is directly evoked by Mark's passage: "He walks on the waves of the sea. . . . If he comes near me, I see him not, if he passes by, I do not recognize him" (Jb 9:8-11).

The disciples think they are seeing a ghost, perhaps one of those "sea demons" which, according to popular fancy, inhabited the deep. The words with which Jesus reassures them can mean "It is I"—that is, the kind of identification of self which anyone might give a friend in the dark. But the literal Greek "I am" can also point to a divine identity. "I am" recalls the divine name revealed to Moses (Ex 3:14) and its uses with "fear not" or "take courage" when the Lord reassured his people of his presence and power in their distress (Is 41:4-10, 13; 43:1; 44:2, 8; 45:5, 7; and especially 51:12: "It is I, it is I who comfort you. Can you then fear?"

As soon as Jesus gets into the boat, the wind drops and the sea calms down—a further manifestation of Jesus' power over the elements, like that shown earlier when he calmed the storm (4:39). The turbulent sea is an ancient biblical symbol of chaos which the Lord dispells by his power and his word. The calming of the sea is thus the final element of Jesus' theophany.

For Mark, then, this event is a manifestation of Jesus' character as Son of God (1:1). Not so for the disciples, who are still resisting the revelation of Jesus' identity. The curious connection Mark makes with the loaves has to be understood in this light. If they had understood that miracle, they would have had no trouble understanding this one, for the two are of one piece: He who feeds the people in the wilderness is the same Lord who walks on the waves of the sea and says, "It is I."

We would expect this whole incident to occur after the resurrection, when Jesus' defiance of natural laws was a matter of course (see Jn 20:19), when he was often not recognized at first, even by his followers, and when his absence was felt and his comforting presence needed in the struggling community. However, Mark has no difficulty seeing Jesus exercise "resurrection power" before his resurrection, undaunted by his disciples failure to understand. The reader, at least, knows who Jesus is, and he is urged not to harden his heart as the light shines through even more powerful signs.

27

Jesus Liberates God's Word
6:53-7:23

[53]And when they had crossed over, they came to land at Gennesaret, and moored to the shore. [54]And when they got out of the boat, immediately the people recognized him, [55]and ran about the whole neighborhood and began to bring sick people on the pallets to any place where they heard he was. [56]And wherever he came, in villages, cities, or country, they laid the sick in

the market places, and besought him that they might touch even the fringe of his garment; and as many as touched it were made well.

7 Now when the Pharisees gathered together to him, with some of the scribes, who had come from Ierusalem, [2]they saw that some of his disciples ate with hands defiled, that is, unwashed. [3](For the Pharisees, and all the Jews, do not eat unless they wash their hands, observing the tradition of the elders; [4]and when they come from the market place, they do not eat unless they purify themselves; and there are many other traditions which they observe, the washing of cups and pots and vessels of bronze.) [5]And the Pharisees and the scribes asked him, "Why do your disciples not live according to the tradition of the elders, but eat with hands defiled?" [6]And he said to them, "Well did Isaiah prophesy of you hypocrites, as it is written, 'This people honors me with their lips, but their heart is far from me; [7]in vain do they worship me, teaching as doctrines the precepts of men.' [8]You leave the commandment of God, and hold fast the tradition of men." [9]And he said to them, "You have a fine way of rejecting the commandment of God, in order to keep your tradition! [10]For Moses said, 'Honor your father and your mother'; and, 'He who speaks evil of father or mother, let him surely die'; [11]but you say, 'If a man tells his father or his mother, What you would have gained from me is Corban, (that is, given to God)— [12]then you no longer permit him to do anything for his father or mother, *[13]thus making void the word of God through your tradition which you hand on. And many such things you do."

[14]And he called the people to him again, and said to them, "Hear me, all of you, and understand: [15]there is nothing outside a man which by going into him can defile him; but the things which come out of a man are what defile him." [17]And when he had entered the

house, and left the people, his disciples asked him about the parable. [18]And he said to them, "Then are you also without understanding? Do you not see that whatever goes into a man from outside cannot defile him, [19]since it enters, not his heart but his stomach, and so passes on?" (Thus he declared all foods clean.) [20]And he said, "What comes out of a man is what defiles a man. [21]For from within, out of the heart of man, come evil thoughts, fornication, theft, murder, adultery, [22]coveting, wickedness, deceit, licentiousness, envy, slander, pride, foolishness. [23]All these evil things come from within, and they defile a man."

ON LANDING AT Gennesaret, Jesus is again besieged by the crowds. He brings God's healing, and people seek to touch even the fringe of his garment. The reader begins to share in the excitement of the good news taking place before his very eyes.

And then, without warning, the reader is plunged into controversy. There is no connecting link between this dispute and the preceding excitement over healing, but by putting these scenes side by side Mark underscores all the more starkly the triviality of the preoccupations of the Pharisees and the scribes. Jesus' focus is on healing, theirs on hand washing.

In the written law, the ritual of hand washing was required only of the priests before entering the sanctuary (Ex 30:19; 40:12). But by Jesus' time many Jews, wishing to imitate priestly holiness, washed their hand daily before morning prayer. The practice of washing before eating bread also evolved. The intention of this practice, as well as of all others in the oral tradition, was to sanctify the whole of daily life. By Jesus' time these traditions, promoting and even guaranteeing the holiness of daily life, had become law for the Pharisees.

The presence here of scribes from Jerusalem betrays the growing concern of the legal experts of Judaism to preserve the oral law from the threat which Jesus and his disciples posed to it. The scribes raise the question about hand washing, but it is obvious from their question, as well as from Mark's explanation for his Roman audience in verse 5, that the issue is really the authority of the whole oral law itself. Jesus replies with a text of Isaiah that goes, literally, to the heart of the question: When external observance gets in the way of true religion, it becomes idolatry—that is, a system of human teachings passed off as God's word.

Jesus pursues the point by another example. He quotes the commandment to honor parents, first in its positive form from Exodus 20:12 and Deuteronomy 5:16, then in its negative form from Exodus 21:17 and Leviticus 20:9. He then points to the oral tradition of Corban. By declaring his goods Corban, that is, dedicated to God, an individual could withdraw all support due his parents, even if he did not subsequently give these goods to the temple but kept them for his own use. Should he regret his vow, some scribal opinion held that he was nevertheless bound and could not reverse his decision, supposedly in keeping with Numbers 30:3, which insists a vow must be fulfilled. But this, Jesus says, is to be trapped by biblical literalism into voiding God's word. And this is only one example of a whole system of legalism.

The questioners now disappear into the background as Jesus gives a universal teaching to the crowd. He offers a riddle: What defiles a person is not what goes into him, but what comes out of him. Jesus gives no further explanation of this mysterious statement to the crowds, in keeping with the policy he has adopted of teaching them only with parables (4:11-12). But inside the house (probably a catchword for the community of disciples where fuller revelation is given—see 4:10; 9:28, 33; 10:10), Jesus explains.

Mark's parenthetical remark, "Thus he declared all foods clean," reflects for his Roman community (see Rom 14:14) the Jesus-based principle by which a long struggle in the early church was to be resolved. It was a struggle not only of "clean and unclean" foods but of table fellowship between Jewish and Gentile Christians (see Acts 10, 11, 15; Gal 2).

At our distance it is hard to realize how cataclysmic this principle was. It was over this practical matter, more than over theoretical issues, that Christianity divided from Judaism. It was precisely at this point that Jesus collided with the Pharisaic and scribal interpretation of the law. For a Gentile Christian this was no problem, but for the Jew who chose to believe in Jesus it was a most wrenching experience, for it meant accepting not only a new understanding of the word of God but also an equality of brotherhood with the Gentiles. The areas on which Jew and Gentile would now come together were ethical ones from the heart and not an agreement about what foods they could eat together.

It is not by accident, then, that Mark places this controversy and Jesus' teaching at the center of this whole section, 6:7 to 8:26, introducing Jesus' journey into Gentile territory where he performs a healing for a Gentile woman. The good news is about to break out of Israel.

28

Healer Without Frontiers

7:24-30

[24]And from there he arose and went away to the region of Tyre and Sidon. And he entered a house, and would not have any one know it; yet he could not be hid. [25]But immediately a woman, whose little daughter was possessed by an unclean spirit, heard of him, and came and fell down at his feet, [26]Now the woman was a Greek, a Syrophoenician by birth. And she begged him to cast the demon out of her daughter. [27]And he said to her, "Let the children first be fed, for it is not right to take the children's bread and throw it to the dogs." [28]But she answered him, "Yes, Lord; yet even the dogs under the table eat the children's crumbs." [29]And he

said to her, "For this saying you may go your way; the demon has left your daughter." [30]And she went home, and found the child lying in bed, and the demon gone.

JESUS' LONG DELAYED PLAN to find time and place to rest with his disciples appears attainable only if he leaves Jewish territory. Here, his journey is to what is today known as Lebanon. The journey has no appearance of a mission, for Jesus enters a house and plans to stay there unnoticed. But his reputation has preceded him, probably conveyed by the representatives of Tyre and Sidon who earlier came to Galilee to see him (3:8).

Here the mysterious interplay common in Mark comes to light again. Jesus wishes to remain hidden but no one will let him. Believers "pull" his power out of him and, as it were, force him to reveal himself. In contrast, his disbelieving enemies not only do not experience his power themselves but try to prevent it from reaching others.

A woman intrudes on the privacy of Jesus and falls at his feet in respect and desperation. Mark underlines her Gentile origin with the precise term *Syro*phoenician, distinguishing her country from that part of Phoenicia around Carthage in North Africa. She asks Jesus to cast the demon out of her daughter. Mark gives us no description of the symptoms here as he does in other cases (1:26; 9:18-26), probably to focus solely upon the woman's faith in her encounter with Jesus.

Initially, Jesus' response sounds harsh and disrespectful. At the level of this woman's understanding, however, this need not have been the case. The dogs here are not stray mongrels but house dogs, the pets which were allowed under the table during a meal. To feed these dogs while the family is eating is inappropriate. They should be fed only after the "children" have eaten. The "children" here may refer to the disciples who are reclining and being spiritually fed by Jesus, but more likely it means the people of Israel, frequently referred to in the Bible as children in relation to the Lord (Ex 4:22; Dt 14:1; Hos 11:1, etc.). Jesus would be reaffirming the limitation of his mission to Israel, while not excluding a possible later extension of the blessings of salvation to the Gentiles. The woman catches the meaning of Jesus' metaphor and uses it to her own advantage: Yes, but the dogs under the table don't have to wait for the *crumbs* that fall *during* the meal—and all I want is a crumb!

This response delights Jesus, and he answers her request by healing her daughter at a distance. The faith of a Gentile woman has put to shame both the faithlessness of Jesus' enemies in Israel and the hardheartedness of his own disciples as well.

At the level of Mark's community and his gospel, however, the story assumes yet a deeper meaning. Jesus has just come from a dispute with the scribes and Pharisees over purity regulations and their consequences for table fellowship. For a Jew to enter a Gentile's home—or vice-versa—and, even worse, to share a meal, was to incur defilement: "Whoever eats with an idolater is like a man who eats with a dog" (*Pirqe Eliezer* 29). This attitude explains the extreme reluctance of good Jews, like Peter, to eat with or enter the household of even one so well-disposed to the faith as Cornelius (Acts 10:14, 17-23); it also explains the temporary table-separation between Christian Jews and Gentiles in Antioch (Gal 2:11-14). It was difficult for a Jew to rid himself, even as a Christian, of the old image of Gentiles as "dogs."

Mark's community, where this issue was still creating problems (Rom 14:14), would recognize the woman's entry into the house as an approach to the Christian community ("the house" in Mark is the place for those petitioners well-disposed toward the Lord, 2:1-5; 3:20; 7:24-30), and Jesus' remark to be an intentional, though passing, reinforcement of the kind of objection the Jewish Christian might pose—only to provoke a more brilliant act of faith on the part of a Gentile. The story then would illustrate the admission of the Gentiles to table fellowship with the Jews, founded in this conversation and the favor Jesus once extended to a Gentile. As such it is a fitting sequel to the preceding discussion about ritual purity in 7:1-23 and a reaffirmation of Jesus' role as healer (6:53-56)—a healer now without frontiers—in contrast to those who look to their washed pots to make them acceptable to God.

29

"He Has Done All Things Well"

7:31-37

³¹Then he returned from the region of Tyre, and went through Sidon to the Sea of Galilee, through the region of the Decapolis. ³²And they brought to him a man who was deaf and had an impediment in his speech; and they besought him to lay his hand upon him. ³³And taking him aside from the multitude privately, he put his fingers into his ears, and he spat and touched his tongue; ³⁴and looking up to heaven, he sighed, and said to him, "Ephphatha," that is, "Be opened." ³⁵And his ears were opened, his tongue was released, and he spoke plainly. ³⁶And he charged them to tell no one; but the more he charged them, the more zealously they proclaimed ·it. ³⁷And they were astonished beyond measure, saying, "He has done all things well; he even makes the deaf hear and the dumb speak."

JESUS LEAVES THE Syrophoenician city of Tyre, moves northward up the coast some twenty miles to Sidon, and then apparently cuts back in a southeasterly direction to the eastern side of the Sea of Galilee. He is still in largely pagan territory, though there were also many Jews living in the area. However, whether the deaf-mute and the crowds are Jewish or Gentile is not important to Mark.

His point is that Jesus works a messianic sign which in a single act fulfills two of the signs foretold in Isaiah 35:5-6: "The ears of the deaf shall be unstopped . . . and the tongue of the dumb shall sing for joy." The dumbness here is not absolute but rather, as the Revised Standard Version suggests, a speech defect which prevents the man from communicating in a normal way. Some members of the crowd ask Jesus to touch the man. Physical touch is important in Mark's portrait of Jesus' healing elsewhere, and it also figures importantly in this story, found only in Mark.

Why does Jesus take the man aside from the crowd? Does he seek privacy in order to enter into the man's world and to relate with him in a more fully personal way? Does Jesus want to avoid being identified with other popular healers in the Hellenistic world? Is he trying to minimize the chances of his being proclaimed a political messiah? Does he wish to subordinate his healing ministry to his role as the suffering servant, a role soon to be revealed to the disciples? No fully satisfactory answer has been given, and it may well be a combination of all of these concerns.

Jesus deals with the man "sacramentally" as it were, actually putting his finger into the man's ears and using spittle to touch his tongue. In our highly antiseptic culture, communication by spittle is regarded as offensive. In Jesus' day it was highly esteemed as an instrument of healing. In any case, there is a physical communication, via spittle, from the tongue of Jesus to the bound tongue of the man.

Jesus is not afraid of touch. Nor is he afraid to express emotion, as he did before healing the leper (Mk 1:41; see Jn 11:33, 38). Was this sighing common procedure in healing? Was this a way in which Jesus responded to the presence of evil, turning the situation over to the Father in intercession? Like the travail that is followed by childbirth, Jesus' deep sigh is followed by the words "Be opened"—addressed not to the ears or the tongue but to the person himself.

The miracle takes place. The man hears Jesus and begins to speak normally. Despite Jesus' attempt to keep the miracle quiet, those who see it *proclaim* it (the same word used elsewhere for preaching the gospel). And they end with an exclamation of praise for *all* that Jesus has done, in fulfillment of Isaiah 35.

This confession-proclamation not only ends the story of the deaf-mute but also concludes the whole section which began with a feeding of the crowds in 6:30-44. Mark leads his reader through other signs and a discussion of the Pharisees' teaching to this climactic healing and confession of praise. Now begins another section which repeats the same pattern: a feeding of the crowds (8:1-10), a discussion with the Pharisees and the disciples about signs (8:11-21), and a cure of a blind man (8:22-26) leading up to Peter's confession of Jesus as the Messiah (8:27-30). Thus the praise of the crowds identifying Jesus as the one who fulfills the messianic prophecies of Isaiah 35:5-7 prepares us to hear Peter say explicitly, "You are the Messiah" (8:29). To this new but similarly structured section we turn next.

30

Look Beyond the Bread
8:1-21

8 In those days, when again a great crowd had gathered, and they had nothing to eat, he called his disciples to him, and said to them, ²"I have compassion on the crowd, because they have been with me now three days, and have nothing to eat; ³and if I send them away hungry to their homes, they will faint on the way; and some of them have come a long way." ⁴And his disciples answered him, "How can one feed these men with bread here in the desert?" ⁵And he asked them, "How many loaves have you?" They said, "Seven." ⁶And he commanded the crowd to sit down on the ground; and he took the seven loaves, and having given thanks he broke them and gave them to his disciples to set before the people; and they set them before the crowd. ⁷And they had a few small fish; and having blessed them, he commanded that these also should be set before them. ⁸And they ate, and were satisfied; and they took up the broken pieces left

over, seven baskets full. [9]And there were about four thousand people. [10]And he sent them away; and immediately he got into the boat with his disciples, and went to the district of Dalmanutha.

[11]The Pharisees came and began to argue with him, seeking from him a sign from heaven, to test him. [12]And he sighed deeply in his spirit, and said, "Why does this generation seek a sign? Truly, I say to you, no sign shall be given to this generation." [13]And he left them, and getting into the boat again he departed to the other side.

[14]Now they had forgotten to bring bread; and they had only one loaf with them in the boat. [15]And he cautioned them, saying, "Take heed, beware of the leaven of the Pharisees and the leaven of Herod." [16]And they discussed it with one another, saying, "We have no bread." [17]And being aware of it, Jesus said to them, "Why do you discuss the fact that you have no bread? Do you not yet perceive or understand? Are your hearts hardened? [18]Having eyes do you not see, and having ears do you not hear? And do you not remember? [19]When I broke the five loaves for the five thousand, how many baskets full of broken pieces did you take up?" They said to him, "Twelve." [20]"And the seven for the four thousand, how many baskets full of broken pieces did you take up?" And they said to him, "Seven." [21]And he said to them, "Do you not yet understand?"

THE FIRST SURPRISE we find in this story of feeding is that Mark should relate it at all. The evangelists are usually quite selective in the miracle stories they report, and generally they avoid relating stories of the same kind unless they have a specific reason for doing so. Earlier in his gospel, Mark gave a graphic picture of Jesus feeding the crowds (6:32-44). Now we have a second feeding story with many similarities to the first: the need of a large crowd in the wilderness moves Jesus to compassion; the supplies of bread and fish are inadequate; Jesus blesses them, gives them to the disciples to distribute, and the amazing surplus of scraps witness to the miraculous multiplication.

A closer look, however, reveals important differences: The second story lacks many of the graphic details of setting, and there are important differences in the size of the crowd, the number of available loaves, and of the baskets of scraps. In the earlier story, Jesus' compassion for the crowd moves him first to *teach* them, and he feeds them as an afterthought, so to speak, on the evening of the first day. In this story, the crowd has been listening to Jesus for three days, and he expresses his compassion by meeting their need for food. An even more important difference was already noted by St. Augustine. The crowd of the first feeding was a Jewish crowd. Here the crowd is Gentile, at least in great part, if we take seriously Mark's setting of the story on the eastern side of the Sea of Galilee. The Gentile composition is also hinted at in the expression, "some of them have come from afar" (v. 3).

So it will not do to say that we have here simply a different version of the same feeding story as it was remembered, per-haps, in another tradition. In 8:19-20, Jesus will remind his disciples of two feedings, not one. At the level of Mark's com-position, certainly, the lesson is different from what was taught in the first story. This story anticipates the welcoming of the Gentiles into table fellowship with Jews in the community of the church. The eucharistic overtones of the passage are even stronger here than before—Mark uses *eucharistesas* ("he gave thanks") instead of *eulogesen* ("he blessed"). The real miracle is not the multiplication of food as such, but the fact that the meal makes of a crowd a community, of Jew and Gentile a brotherhood.

Abruptly the scene flashes to the other side of the lake, where the Pharisees ask Jesus for a "sign from heaven to test him." The narrative is again moving at two levels. In the life situation of Jesus, the Pharisees do not consider the miracles of Jesus as authentic signs that he is from God. Miracles can be ambiguous, as Deuteronomy 13:1-3 warned, and the scribes had already decided that Jesus was working by the devil's power (3:22-30). The Pharisees now ask him for the kind of sign from God which would test this "prophet" and convince them beyond all doubt that he was from God. Jesus is thoroughly exasperated, and he responds to them in language echoing the solemn oaths of the Old Testament. What they really want is something that would excuse them from faith and a change of heart. The works and teachings of Jesus are sufficient for those open to God's revelation. To ask for more in the face of these is not to test the prophet, but to test God. Further discussion would be useless, so Jesus again gets into the boat and departs for the other side of the lake.

At the level of Mark's teaching, placing this demand for a sign immediately after the feeding of the multitudes highlights the importance of understanding and responding to this and all of Jesus' miracles in the light of faith. It is an important lesson for the disciples.

But the disciples themselves have not proven immune to the dullness of the Pharisees and Herod, who are more interested in signs than in really knowing and confessing who Jesus is. In their haste they have forgotten to take bread for the trip. Jesus warns them of the "leaven," that is, the corrosive attitude, of the sign-seekers. Hearing only "leaven" and understanding it as a literal reference to bread, the disciples quarrel among themselves about their lack of it, thoroughly forgetting that he who multiplied the loaves is with them in the boat. In fact, the boat is actually well supplied for the journey if it has the "one bread" who is Jesus (see 1 Cor 10:17). The disciples as yet do not understand what they have witnessed: They are blind and deaf like the others. But this situation is only temporary, for Jesus is gradually bringing them to a knowledge of his true identity.

"I Was Blind But Now I See!"

8:22-30

²²And they came to Beth-saida. And some people brought to him a blind man, and begged him to touch him. ²³And he took the blind man by the hand, and led him out of the village; and when he had spit on his eyes and laid his hands upon him, he asked him, "Do you see anything?" ²⁴And he looked up and said, "I see men; but they look like trees, walking." ²⁵Then again he laid his hands upon his eyes; and he looked intently and was restored, and saw everything clearly. ²⁶And he sent him away to his home, saying, "Do not even enter the village."

²⁷And Jesus went on with his disciples, to the villages of Caesarea Philippi; and on the way he asked his disciples, "Who do men say that I am?" ²⁸And they told him, "John the Baptist; and others say, Elijah; and others one of the prophets." ²⁹And he asked them, "But who do you say that I am?" Peter answered him, "You are the Christ." ³⁰And he charged them to tell no one about him.

JESUS HAS JUST upbraided his disciples for being spiritually blind and deaf—that is, for lacking understanding of who he is (8:17-20). Now, at Bethsaida, on the northwest side of the lake, he works an unusual miracle, recorded only by Mark. He heals a blind man progressively. Not only is the story a lesson about persistent prayer for healing, the importance of physical touch, or even Jesus' power to heal in general. It is a parable in action of what Jesus is doing for his disciples. He is gradually leading them out of *their* blindness, step by step, to see who he really is.

This teaching function of the miracle may explain better than anything else what has always puzzled interpreters: Why does Jesus lead the man away from the village and forbid him to go back there directly. There is an intimacy about the healing which foreshadows the intimacy on the road to Caesarea Philippi, where Jesus will heal the disciples' blindness in a similar way. There, too, there is a restoring of partial sight (Jesus is a prophet, 8:27-28), followed by full sight (Jesus is the Messiah, 8:30), followed by a command to be silent about the revelation (8:30).

With the incident on the road to Caesarea Philippi, Mark reaches the first crest of his gospel, the point to which everything has been leading thus far. After opening his work with the words, "The beginning of the gospel of Jesus, the Messiah, the Son of God," he has shown Jesus in action and teaching, but nowhere has any human witness guessed his real identity. To his adversaries he is demon-possessed; to the crowds he is Elijah, or an ancient prophet come back; to Herod he is John the Baptist risen from the dead. To the disciples, who have shared his life most intimately, he is still a puzzle; despite all the signs they have seen him work, they do not understand (8:21). Now they will reach their first true insight, forecast in Mark's opening line: "You are the Messiah!"

It is Simon, whom Jesus has renamed Peter (Rock, 3:16), who speaks here, both in his own name and, as elsewhere, for the Twelve (9:5; 10:28; 11:21; 14:29). Though Mark does not tell us explicitly, as Matthew does, that this confession of faith is a gift from the Father alone, the fact is implied by the contrast of Peter's identification with that made by "men," a term Mark often uses for those unable to grasp divine revelation (1:17; 7:7-8; 9:31; 10:27; 11:30).

What does the title "Messiah" mean? Literally, it means "anointed one." Israel's hopes for future salvation took on many forms. There would be a prophet like Moses (Dt 18:15), an anointed messenger (Is 61:1-4), a heavenly deliverer called the Son of Man, who would inaugurate God's rule or kingdom (after Dn 7:13, 18). But the most common stream of future hope centered on the ancient promises made to King David (2 Sm 7:14-16): Through him and through his sons-successors, God would bring salvation to his people. Though applied later to priests and prophets, the term "anointing" was most radically the right of kings and thus "anointed one" came to be a term for the unique King-Son of David who would be Israel's final deliverer.

Though this Messiah was to be righteous, a model of holiness (Is 9:7; 11:1-5), no one doubted that he would be a political leader and not only would the Messiah deliver Israel from all its suffering, but he himself would not suffer. True, there was that "Song of the Suffering Servant" in Isaiah 52-53, but no one ever thought of the Messiah in such terms—or if they did, the "being crushed" was applied to the enemies of the Messiah, not to the Messiah himself.

The fate of Jesus, and his understanding of this role of the Messiah, only vaguely alluded to up to this point in Mark (2:20; 3:6), will become the major theme of the gospel from this point on. Since Jesus' understanding of his role as Messiah differs so sharply from the people's and even from his own disciples', his command to keep his identity quiet is understandable. Peter knows the right words but still has to learn what they really mean.

The whole section from 6:32 to 8:30 now falls into place. Jesus feeds a Jewish crowd (6:32-44), then after other miracles (6:45-56) replaces the teaching of the scribes and Pharisees (7:1-23), heals a Gentile (7:24-30), and then a deaf-mute, leading to the crowd's hymn of praise confessing him as wonderworker (7:31-37). A second series begins with another feeding, this time of a Jewish-Gentile crowd (8:1-10), followed by a dispute with the Pharisees about signs (8:11-13), carrying over into a diagnosing of the disciples' similar spiritual blindness (8:14-21), then the gradual healing of a blind man (8:22-26), which prepares for the healing of the disciples' blindness in their confession of Jesus' identity (8:27-30).

The Christian reader is offered the challenge given to the crowds and the disciples: You have seen and heard. Will you allow Jesus to heal your blindness and loose your tongue so you also can confess him as God's envoy, the Messiah?

32

A Suffering Messiah?

8:31-33

[31]And he began to teach them that the Son of man must suffer many things, and be rejected by the elders and the chief priests and the scribes, and be killed, and after three days rise again. [32]And he said this plainly. And Peter took him, and began to rebuke him. [33]But turning and seeing his disciples, he rebuked Peter, and said, "Get behind me, Satan! For you are not on the side of God, but of men."

WITH THE OPENING line of this passage, Mark wants us to know that an entirely new stage of Jesus' life, ministry, and teaching begins. Up to this point the reader has shared the disciples' amazement at his work and teaching. With them he has come to discover who Jesus is—a prophet and more than a prophet, the Messiah. Now, however, there is a shock. The word "Messiah" doesn't mean to Jesus what it means to the disciples. In fact, Jesus even avoids the term and substitutes another, "Son of Man."

"Son of Man" was sometimes just a way of saying "I," and on the lips of Jesus at this point it may have meant nothing more. On the other hand, it is clear elsewhere in Mark that "Son of Man" stands for the glorious figure in Daniel 7:13-14: "Behold, with the clouds of heaven there came one like a son of man, and he came to the Ancient of Days [God] and was presented before him. And to him was given dominion and glory and kingdom, that all peoples, nations, and languages should serve him; his dominion is an everlasting dominion, which shall not pass away, and his kingdom one that shall not be destroyed." Daniel is told further on that this "son of man" stands for the holy people of God to whom God will give the final victory over the forces of evil (7:18). But in the developing tradition represented in the noncanonical Book of Enoch, this figure is understood to be an individual, and he is identified with the Messiah. Jesus, or at least Mark, may have been building on that tradition. If so, there was nothing in the tradition either about the Messiah or the Son of Man that predicted suffering for him. Where did this notion come from? Obviously, it was some kind of direct revelation given by the Father to Jesus, but it also involved Jesus' reading of both the trends of his ministry and certain Old Testament passages. This process, begun by Jesus, was enriched by the ongoing experience and meditation of the early church, to which Mark himself was both heir and contributor. Let's look at verse 31 in detail:

"The Son of man must suffer many things." On the screen of the popular view of the Messiah, Jesus flashes a shocking overlay—the picture of the suffering servant in Isaiah 52:13-53:12, who bears the sins "of the many."

"He will be rejected." This not only predicts the future but echoes Psalm 118:22 (the stone rejected by the builders), which Jesus later quotes in Mark 12:10.

"By the elders, the chief priests, and the scribes." These are the authorities in Jerusalem and their "theologians," who support them with scriptural justification for their position.

"And be killed." Jesus does not mention the cross here, though it can be inferred from 8:34. It is sufficient at this first prediction of the passion to foretell his death by violence, as Isaiah had prophesied (53:8).

"And after three days rise again." Even in this element of the prediction there is an echo of an Old Testament text about the consolation of Israel after a time of suffering: "Come, let us return to the Lord, for he has torn that he may heal us; he has stricken, and he will bind us up. After two days he will revive us; *on the third day he will raise us up* that we may have life before him" (Hos 6:1-2). In the first century, "he will raise us up" was interpreted literally as the resurrection of the dead. Thus Jesus' prediction of his suffering was not a message of pessimism or of gloom regarding the ultimate outcome of his ministry. It *was* a shocking announcement, on the basis of Isaiah 52-53, of *how* the final victory would be achieved.

Mark notes that he said this plainly—that is, no longer in the allusive speech of parables (4:11-12). Peter's response indicates that he, and probably the rest of the disciples, understood what Jesus meant. Peter begins to rebuke Jesus. What a strong word for Mark to use here—the same word he uses to describe Jesus rebuking the demon! Obviously Peter's response is a strong, emotional one. But Jesus in turn rebukes Peter. The same term is used again as Jesus identifies the invitation to be from Satan, who had tested him in the desert (1:13) and through the questioning by his enemies (8:11; 10:2; 12:15). Jesus has to face Satan even in the blindness of his chief disciple!

The message is perfectly clear: Jesus is to take the role assigned him by the Father. He will not follow the script written by men or by Satan.

Twice again in Mark Jesus will predict the passion (9:31; 10:31-32). These three predictions form the backbone of the whole section 8:31 to 10:52, which concerns Jesus' journey to Jerusalem, the cross, and the more intimate instruction of the disciples, who, despite the repetition, never understand or accept the new teaching. Of the fourteen Son of Man sayings in Mark, these three concerning his suffering are balanced by three predicting his glory (8:38; 13:26; 14:62). But Jesus will attain that glory, as will his disciples, only by first walking the way of the cross.

33

Cross Before Me, World Behind Me

8:34-9:1

³⁴And he called to him the multitude with his disciples, and said to them, "If any man would come after me, let him deny himself and take up his cross and follow me. ³⁵For whoever would save his life will lose it; and whoever loses his life for my sake and the gospel's will save it. ³⁶For what does it profit a man, to gain the whole world and forfeit his life? ³⁷For what can a man give in return for his life? ³⁸For whoever is ashamed of me and of my words in this adulterous and sinful generation, of him will the Son of man also be ashamed, when he comes in the glory of his Father with the holy angels."

9 And he said to them, "Truly, I say to you, there are some standing here who will not taste death before they see the kingdom of God come with power."

JESUS HAS JUST told his disciples that his path to glory is through suffering and death (8:31-33). Might his disciples rejoice at least that such a lot would be spared them? Some in Mark's Roman community may have hoped so. Others may have defected when the cross they had revered now faced them as the instrument of their own persecution and execution.

These sayings of Jesus are directed not only at the intimate disciples who would become the leaders of Mark's community but at everyone who follows Jesus. This seems to be the reason for Mark's surprising note that Jesus calls the crowds with the disciples to hear this word. No one is exempted.

"To deny" is a courtroom term in which a witness disavows any association with another. "To deny oneself" means that one has broken with all self-interest. The "old self" is no longer recognized as having any rights. "To take up his cross" must have shocked the Jewish crowds who first heard this word, for it evoked not only the cruelest of Roman executions but the stigma of being an outlaw. By the time Mark's community heard the word, of course, they knew exactly what it meant: The kind of death Jesus had suffered they too must be ready to undergo.

The stark paradox of verse 35 needs no commentary. To save one's life one must lose it. What is now crystal clear for the first time, however, is that the gospel is not merely a message preached *by* Jesus. It is identical with Jesus himself: "for my sake and the gospel's." This expression is a catchword in Mark (8:35; 10:29). From this point on, the "gospel" means not Jesus' preaching of the kingdom (1:14-15) but the message *about Jesus* which the church proclaims (see also 13:10; 14:9).

Jesus drives the point home with business language. What value is there in gaining the whole world if the price you pay is your own eternal life (vv. 36-37)? Finally, he points out the ill-starred logic of the apostate disciple. If he is foolish enough to be ashamed of Jesus and his words before "this adulterous and sinful generation" (a term echoing the prophets' condemnation of idolatry, Ez 16:32; Hos 2:4), then the Son of Man (Jesus as victorious judge) will in turn be ashamed of him at the final judgment.

The last verse of this section (9:1) has been a puzzle for interpreters. It seems that Jesus is promising his return in glory during the lifetime of some of his listeners. This is how many early Christians appear to have understood it. However, Mark's placement of the statement here, immediately before the transfiguration, points to a different interpretation. The present generation of Jesus' followers may indeed be called upon to suffer and even to die for their Lord, but some of them will be granted, even before their death, a vision of the kingdom of God coming in glory, namely, the transfiguration.

Is such an understanding of this passage justified? In the transfiguration, Jesus is certainly described with the imagery of the parousia (9:7; 14:62), and the disciples are forbidden to tell what happened until after the resurrection (9:9). Moreover, a look at 2 Peter 1:16-18 shows us that the transfiguration was understood to be an anticipated parousia: "We made known to you the *power* and the *coming* of our Lord Jesus Christ, . . . we were eyewitnesses of his majesty. For when he received honor and glory from God the Father and the voice was borne to him by the majestic Glory, 'This is my beloved Son, with whom I am well pleased,' we heard this voice borne from heaven, for we were with him on the holy mountain."

There are other indications that Mark understood the prophecy to be fulfilled in the transfiguration. Right after the prophecy, Mark introduces the vision by the words, "Six days later" which gives a clear temporal connection with the prophecy. Also, the verb *see* in 9:1 occurs again in 9:9 as a kind of fulfillment indicator. In spite of the cross and persecution that will hang over all the disciples as it did over Jesus, a select few of the present company, Peter, James, and John, will see the kingdom in power. This vision, as the text from 2 Peter shows, will be enough to sustain the rest of the suffering disciples in their hope.

34

Jesus Transfigured

9:2-13

²And after six days Jesus took with him Peter and James and John, and led them up a high mountain apart by themselves; and he was transfigured before them, ³and his garments became glistening, intensely

white, as no fuller on earth could bleach them. [4]And there appeared to them Elijah with Moses; and they were talking to Jesus. [5]And Peter said to Jesus, "Master, it is well that we are here; let us make three booths, one for you and one for Moses and one for Elijah." [6]For he did not know what to say, for they were exceedingly afraid. [7]And a cloud overshadowed them, and a voice came out of the cloud, "This is my beloved Son; listen to him." [8]And suddenly looking around they no longer saw any one with them but Jesus only.

[9]And as they were coming down the mountain, he charged them to tell no one what they had seen, until the Son of man should have risen from the dead. [10]So they kept the matter to themselves, questioning what the rising from the dead meant. [11]And they asked him, "Why do the scribes say that first Elijah must come?" [12]And he said to them, "Elijah does come first to restore all things; and how is it written of the Son of man, that he should suffer many things and be treated with contempt? [13]But I tell you that Elijah has come, and they did to him whatever they pleased, as it is written of him.

FOR ONE WHO reads this passage without a deep knowledge of the Old Testament and a prior knowledge of the resurrection of Jesus, its meaning is likely to remain as obscure as it was for the disciples. Exodus 24:12-18 bears reading at this point. There Moses takes a companion and goes up the mountain. After six days of preparation he hears the voice of God speaking in an all-covering cloud, and the glory of God is revealed in a magnificent theophany. Though there are several differences between this event and the transfiguration, the similarities tell us, as they would tell any Jewish reader, that God is bringing the whole meaning of the Old Testament law (Moses) and the prophets (Elijah) to fulfillment in Jesus—as had indeed been promised by Deuteronomy 18:15.

Peter still shows his lack of understanding by addressing Jesus as "Rabbi" and proposing to house the three heavenly figures with tents—a faint parallel with the Exodus account in which Moses is told, after the theophany of 24:12-18, to build a tent for the Lord's dwelling (25-27). Yet the event itself also gives a foretaste of the glory of Jesus' resurrection and the second coming: Jesus' garments are dazzling white as befits his risen glory (see 16:6); the cloud will be the vehicle of his second coming (14:62); and the chosen disciples see the kingdom of God coming in power (9:1).

According to Luke, Moses and Elijah were discussing Jesus' impending departure, his own "exodus" soon to occur in Jerusalem, that is, his death and resurrection (Lk 9:31). Mark is not so explicit, but the voice out of the cloud, reveals to the disciples what at his baptism was confided to Jesus alone (1:11)—not only that Jesus is God's son but that they should listen to him. This must be understood in the light of Jesus' teaching about his own suffering and the share his disciples will have in it. Jesus is the "prophet-like-Moses" to whom, raised up, the people must listen (Dt 18:15). But Jesus is more—God's very own son, who reveals the person and the will of God. He must be listened to even when he speaks of humiliation and suffering.

Moses and Elijah vanish, leaving Jesus to go to the cross alone. Yet this day of glory has been forever seared on the memories of the disciples as a deep mystical experience of the twofold pattern foretold in Isaiah: The Lord's servant will be glorified (52:13-15) but only after suffering and death (53:1-12).

Why does Jesus charge the disciples to keep the experience secret for the time being? Probably because they still neither understand nor accept his suffering role. They would ignore this point in their broadcasting and kindle even more the people's hopes that Jesus would be the type of humanly victorious Messiah they wanted. The "until" of verse 9, however, is crucial: The day will come when they will preach Jesus as risen from the dead and coming in the Father's glory.

The disciples do not question what "rising from the dead" means in general, but what it means for *Jesus*. Why should he have to experience death *before* rising to glory? Elijah, after all, was carried up into glory without being put to death. And if, according to Malachi 4:5-6 and the interpretation of the scribes, Elijah was to restore all things before the coming of the Messiah in glory, there would be no further work for the Messiah to do except to enter into his glory.

"Elijah has already come," asserts Jesus, and in the parallel passage in Matthew, the disciples understand him to mean John the Baptist (Mt 17:13). John came as Elijah, not only in his ascetic life-style and preaching of repentance, but also in his suffering at the hands of an unscrupulous queen and a weak king (Jezebel-Ahab/Herodias-Herod Antipas). The people in power not only refused to convert but persecuted the prophet as well; though sent by God to restore all things, he was frustrated in his work and put to a violent death. One should expect no different a lot for Jesus, even though he is God's son and will one day return in the Father's glory.

35

The Power of Faith and Prayer

9:14-29

[14]And when they came to the disciples, they saw a great crowd about them, and scribes arguing with them. [15]And immediately all the crowd, when they saw him, were greatly amazed, and ran up to him and greeted him. [16]And he asked them, "What are you discussing with them?" [17]And one of the crowd answered him, "Teacher, I brought my son to you, for he has a dumb spirit; [18]and wherever it seizes him, it dashes him down; and he foams and grinds his teeth and becomes rigid; and I asked your disciples to cast it out, and they were not able." [19]And he answered them, "O

faithless generation, how long am I to be with you? How long am I to bear with you? Bring him to me." [20]And they brought the boy to him; and when the spirit saw him, immediately it convulsed the boy, and he fell on the ground and rolled about, foaming at the mouth. [21]And Jesus asked his father, "How long has he had this?" And he said, "From childhood. [22]And it has often cast him into the fire and into the water, to destroy him; but if you can do anything, have pity on us and help us." [23]And Jesus said to him, "If you can! All things are possible to him who believes." [24]Immediately the father of the child cried out and said, "I believe; help my unbelief!" [25]And when Jesus saw that a crowd came running together, he rebuked the unclean spirit, saying to it, "You dumb and deaf spirit, I command you, come out of him, and never enter him again." [26]And after crying out and convulsing him terribly, it came out, and the boy was like a corpse; so that most of them said, "He is dead." [27]But Jesus took him by the hand and lifted him up, and he arose. [28]And when he had entered the house, his disciples asked him privately, "Why could we not cast it out?" [29]And he said to them, "This kind cannot be driven out by anything but prayer."

AFTER THE TRANSFIGURATION, Jesus and the three disciples approach the remaining disciples, only to find them disputing with the scribes and surrounded by a crowd. The scribes represent the Jerusalem authorities, who are keeping Jesus under close surveillance. They will have an important role to play in the last act of the gospel, but Mark simply notes their presence here (Matthew, and Luke do not) without making it crucial to the story itself.

The people are amazed just at the sight of Jesus and run to greet him, an action one might expect of the disciples after the resurrection or at the parousia. Is Mark suggesting, at one level of his account, that Jesus would give this lesson on prayer if he were to return now to Mark's community, which is lacking power in its deliverance ministry?

The story is full of graphic detail and surprises. Jesus asks them (either the scribes or his disciples) what they are discussing, but before they can answer, a man from the crowd blurts the story out. The symptoms are those of epilepsy, but behind them the power of evil is at work, keeping the child in real bondage and even threatening his life. The boy's father, assuming that the disciples had Jesus' power, judged that bringing the boy to them was equivalent to bringing him to Jesus. Jesus' exasperated rebuke is apparently addressed not to the father but to the disciples, whom he here momentarily associates with the disbelievers who want signs without faith.

The encounter of the spirit with Jesus convulses the child and leads Jesus to ask the father how long the child has suffered this bondage. The question allows the father to further expand on the dreadful effects of the spirit's presence. He then says, "If you can do anything, have pity on us and help us." The plural *us* means that Jesus' intervention would benefit not only the boy but the boy's family and village as well. It also echoes the liturgical prayer now become common in Mark's community: "Have pity on us and help us."

The father's question, however, is a kind of left-handed compliment. Frustrated at the failure of the disciples, he does not give Jesus much more room than he gave them. He is like those people who come for healing almost as a test and not because they believe anything will happen. "I've been prayed for before and nothing happened."

Jesus sees that the father first needs to be healed of his lack of faith. "If you can" can be understood with the stress either on *can* ("so you have doubts as to whether I can?") or with the stress on *you* ("it's not a question of whether I can but whether you can. If you believe, all things are possible, even this"). The challenge works. The father answers with a shout that both affirms his belief and yet shows he is aware that he needs Jesus' help even to believe adequately. The man, even in believing, does not rely on his own faith but solely on Jesus (a great lesson to remember when we pray for healing!).

Jesus responds to the father's cry. He also sees a larger crowd gathering and does not want fanfare and publicity to block his real mission. As he is driving the spirit out, the boy is convulsed the third time, more violently than before. The result of this last round with the evil spirit is that there is a mini death-and-resurrection scene, certainly intended by Mark. The boy appears dead, but Jesus lifts him up and he arises (as Jesus himself one day will do). The careful choice of words here allows Mark's theology to shine through: Satan's last triumph will be the death of Jesus, but the victory is only apparent. Jesus will rise victorious, and Satan's power will be definitively broken.

The conclusion to the story is a lesson for the disciples. Jesus had indeed given them the power to cast out demons, and they had used it with success (6:7, 13). But apparently they had assumed that the power was at their command without needing their own faith-reliance on Jesus, the source of it. The church of Mark's day—and ours—is being told that its charismatic power is not to be taken for granted. Ministry must be backed by a powerhouse of prayer.

36

The Rough Road of Discipleship
9:30-50

[30]They went on from there and passed through Galilee. And he would not have any one know it; [31]for he was teaching his disciples, saying to them, "The Son of man will be delivered into the hands of men, and they will kill him; and when he is killed, after three days he will rise." [32]But they did not understand the saying, and they were afraid to ask him.

[33]And they came to Capernaum; and when he was in the house he asked them, "What were you discussing

on the way?" [34]But they were silent; for on the way they had discussed with one another who was the greatest. [35]And he sat down and called the twelve; and he said to them, "If any one would be first, he must be last of all and servant of all." [36]And he took a child, and put him in the midst of them; and taking him in his arms, he said to them, [37]"Whoever receives one such child in my name receives me; and whoever receives me, receives not me but him who sent me."

[38]John said to him, "Teacher, we saw a man casting out demons in your name, and we forbade him, because he was not following us." [39]But Jesus said, "Do not forbid him; for no one who does a mighty work in my name will be able soon after to speak evil of me. [40]For he that is not against us is for us. [41]For truly, I say to you, whoever gives you a cup of water to drink because you bear the name of Christ, will by no means lose his reward.

[42]"Whoever causes one of these little ones who believe in me to sin, it would be better for him if a great millstone were hung round his neck and he were thrown into the sea. [43]And if your hand causes you to sin, cut it off; it is better for you to enter life maimed than with two hands to go to hell, to the unquenchable fire. [45]And if your foot causes you to sin, cut it off; it is better for you to enter life lame than with two feet to be thrown into hell. [47]And if your eye causes you to sin, pluck it out; it is better for you to enter the kingdom of God with one eye than with two eyes to be thrown into hell, [48]where their worm does not die, and the fire is not quenched. [49]For every one will be salted with fire. [50]Salt is good; but if the salt has lost its saltness, how will you season it? Have salt in yourselves, and be at peace with one another."

JESUS PASSES AGAIN through Galilee, but this time it is not healing, driving out demons, and preaching to the crowds that command his activity. We are given the impression that he is now avoiding the crowds (9:25). Jesus is walking in the shadow of the cross, and his energy is spent entirely on his disciples. A second time Jesus foretells his passion, this time using the expression "delivered up [or, "handed over"] into the hands of men." It recalls Jeremiah's danger of being put to death by the people (Jer 26:24). For Jesus, the hands of men are, of course, the authorities, and Judas is the one who hands him over (14:18, 21). But by using the passive verb form here, Mark may well be suggesting that it is God "who did not spare his own Son but handed him over for the sake of us all" (Rom 8:32). Even after this second prediction, the disciples do not understand, and fear keeps them from wanting to know more.

The chapter ends with a number of sayings on discipleship addressed privately ("in the house") to his followers. They are probably independent sayings of Jesus drawn from different situations and are brought together not by reason of their subject matter but by a process called *catchword composition*. Today we do not find this method of organizing a homily easy to follow. On the lips of some preachers it even amuses, as when the pastor of a Catholic parish announced, "Today is the feast of St. Joseph. St. Joseph was a carpenter. Carpenters build confessionals. And confessions will be heard tonight at eight o'clock." But for the early preachers of the gospel, it was one way of organizing and memorizing sayings of Jesus. The word-chain in this series is: servant-child (the same word stands for both in Aramaic)/name/little one/scandal/fire/salt/peace. Note, however, that there is some consistency in the series, at least in the fact that the listener is brought back at the end to the topic introduced at the beginning—from rivalry to peace.

The meaning of Jesus' teaching on leadership is clear: Seek to be last of all and servant of all. But the Christian *talya* (Aramaic) is not merely a servant; he is also a child (the same Aramaic word). And just as Jesus embraces the child, so whoever receives the disciple will be receiving and welcoming Jesus and, in Jesus, the Father who sent him (9:37). The welcomer may be another disciple, or simply one who offers a first gesture of hospitality to the Christian missionary (see v. 41), or one who listens to his preaching.

The same measure of openness is to be shown those who work in Jesus' name, even though they may not join the company of the disciples. The question about the strange exorcist is raised by John—the only time John is singled out as a questioner in Mark. God can work outside even his own established channels, and he sometimes does, as in this case (see also Nm 11:16-30). Problems in applying this principle to new situations in the church will lead Matthew to drop the saying entirely and Luke to report how the itinerant Jewish exorcists' attempt to use Jesus' name ended in their own brutal defeat (Acts 19:13-16).

If the Christian missionary is so precious in God's eyes that anyone who gives him a drink will not lose his reward (v. 41), the reverse holds for those who lead any disciple into sin (9:42). A millstone could weigh as much as a ton! The disciple himself should realize his own preciousness in God's eyes and be willing to undergo any sacrifice to avoid sin (9:43-48). Though the comparisons are Jewish hyperbole, one thinks of Christians like Maria Goretti who suffered martyrdom rather than violate her consecration to the Lord, or Thomas More who could have saved his life had he compromised his conscience before King Henry VIII.

The imagery of the worm and the fire for eternal punishment is drawn from Jewish tradition represented by Judith 16:17 and Sirach 7:17.

"Fire" is a catchword leading to "salt." The salt of verses 49 and 50 is the salt used with victims offered on the altar. We are no longer in the imagery of punishment but rather of purification and preservation. The disciples of Jesus who remain faithful may have to suffer and even die like their master. To be totally committed with their lives, to be willing to die the death of martyrs is not only to "prove one's salt." It also banishes petty ambitions and rivalries (9:34). There is no deeper bond of unity than that between those who face death together for Jesus' sake. Be willing to do that and perfect peace will be yours.

37

Marriage and Children

10:1-16

10 And he left there and went to the region of Judea and beyond the Jordan, and crowds gathered to him again; and again, as his custom was, he taught them. ²And Pharisees came up and in order to test him asked, "Is it lawful for a man to divorce his wife?" ³He answered them, "What did Moses command you?" ⁴They said, "Moses allowed a man to write a certificate of divorce, and to put her away." ⁵But Jesus said to them, "For your hardness of heart he wrote you this commandment. ⁶But from the beginning of creation, 'God made them male and female.' ⁷For this reason a man shall leave his father and mother and be joined to his wife, ⁸and the two shall become one flesh.' So they are no longer two but one flesh. ⁹What therefore God has joined together, let not man put asunder."

¹⁰And in the house the disciples asked him again about this matter. ¹¹And he said to them, "Whoever divorces his wife and marries another, commits adultery against her; ¹²and if she divorces her husband and marries another, she commits adultery."

¹³And they were bringing children to him, that he might touch them; and the disciples rebuked them. ¹⁴But when Jesus saw it he was indignant, and said to them, "Let the children come to me, do not hinder them; for to such belongs the kingdom of God. ¹⁵Truly, I say to you, whoever does not receive the kingdom of God like a child shall not enter it." ¹⁶And he took them in his arms and blessed them, laying his hands upon them.

JESUS LEAVES GALILEE for the last time and begins the long journey to Jerusalem, traveling through the mountains of Samaria to Judea, and then crossing to the eastern side of the Jordan. After a period of retirement in Galilee, he resumes his public teaching in the territory where John the Baptist denounced Herod for his adulterous union with Herodias, a denouncement that ultimately cost John his life. It is a perfect setting for the Pharisees to set a trap for Jesus by raising the same issue! With good reason, Mark notes that it is more than a theoretical question: They are testing Jesus, as did Satan in the desert (1:13).

In Deuteronomy 24:1, a man who found "something unclean," that is, shameful, in his wife was permitted to divorce her, provided he gave her a written notice of her dismissal as public proof of her freedom to marry another man. The question concerning what constituted something unclean was debated between the two rabbinical schools: that of Shammai limited it to something moral or religious in nature, and that of Hillel allowed practically anything that annoyed the husband.

Jesus cuts through all casuistry, going to the intention of the law they cite, and even beyond it to the divine intention for marriage. The purpose of the permission was certainly not to promote divorce; rather, accepting an evil situation, the law sought to protect the wife from abuse and to assure her rights. Divorce itself, however, does not correspond to God's original intention for the married couple. They are, in his mind, one flesh, and man does not have the right to separate what God has bonded together.

What may have remained mysterious for the crowds Jesus makes clear to his disciples privately. Divorce amounts to adultery. In the phrase "commits adultery against her" the emphasis falls on the words "against her." In Jewish law, a man could only commit adultery against another man (by having relations with the latter's wife). He could not commit adultery against his wife, though she, by extra-marital sex, could commit adultery against him. Jesus' interpretation of the Genesis text means there is a personal union in the marriage bond which elevates the woman to real equality with her husband. For a man to break that unity is to sin against her.

The woman, however, is also bound. Though Jewish women were not permitted to initiate divorce, there were cases where a woman deserted her husband to live with and even marry another. Herodias is a case in point. Jesus brands this act as adultery.

By New Testament times, Roman law permitted women to file for divorce. In the best Greek manuscripts of Mark 10:12, the word is "divorce." Other manuscripts, perhaps reflecting the more primitive Jewish tradition, have "desert." It is possible that Jesus, alluding to the Jewish situation represented by Herodias, used the word "desert," while Mark, interpreting Jesus' meaning for his Gentile readers, quite appropriately used "divorce," which was a legal possibility in Rome.

Mark does not explain why the disciples tried to prevent children from being brought to Jesus, but it is another example of their misunderstanding of who Jesus is and what he is about. Perhaps they thought the kingdom is only for adults and that children would interfere with the important business of preaching the gospel. Quite the contrary, Jesus flushes with indignation (only Mark gives us this lively detail). Children exhibit acceptance of the *gift* of the kingdom in a way adults do not—they know how to receive. The kingdom is gift, not labor. In this sense every adult must become a child.

Some scholars, Catholic and Protestant, think this story was preserved in the memory of the early church because it helped resolve the question of the baptism of the infant children of Christians. In any case, Jesus finds children no less worthy of his embrace and the kingdom than adults—and, under the circumstances, even more open than his overly-serious and self-concerned disciples.

38

Give to the Poor and Follow Me
10:17-31

[17]And as he was setting out on his journey, a man ran up and knelt before him, and asked him, "Good Teacher, what must I do to inherit eternal life?" [18]And Jesus said to him, "Why do you call me good? No one is good but God alone. [19]You know the commandments: 'Do not kill, Do not commit adultery, Do not steal, Do not bear false witness, Do not defraud, Honor your father and mother.'" [20]And he said to him, "Teacher, all these I have observed from my youth." [21]And Jesus looking upon him loved him, and said to him, "You lack one thing; go, sell what you have, and give to the poor, and you will have treasure in heaven; and come, follow me." [22]At that saying his countenance fell, and he went away sorrowful; for he had great possessions.

[23]And Jesus looked around and said to his disciples, "How hard it will be for those who have riches to enter the kingdom of God!" [24]And the disciples were amazed at his words. But Jesus said to them again, "Children, how hard it is to enter the kingdom of God! [25]It is easier for a camel to go through the eye of a needle than for a rich man to enter the kingdom of God." [26]And they were exceedingly astonished, and said to him, "Then who can be saved?" [27]Jesus looked at them and said, "With men it is impossible, but not with God; for all things are possible with God." [28]Peter began to say to him, "Lo, we have left everything and followed you." [29]Jesus said, "Truly, I say to you, there is no one who has left house or brothers or sisters or mother or father or children or lands, for my sake and for the gospel,

³⁰who will not receive a hundred-fold now in this time, houses and brothers and sisters and mothers and children and lands, with persecutions, and in the age to come eternal life. ³¹But many that are first will be last, and the last first."

JESUS HAS JUST dealt with ambition as an obstacle to entering the kingdom, holding up a child as model for receiving the gift (10:13-16). Now, resuming his journey to Jerusalem (10:17) and preparing to predict his passion a third time (10:32-34), Jesus deals with another obstacle: wealth, both spiritual and material.

A man of obviously good disposition runs up to Jesus, drops to his knees in reverence, and salutes him with an address never used otherwise in Jewish practice: "Good teacher." Jesus detects in the man an anxiety to cling to Jesus as a new source of spiritual wealth, and he directs the man's attention to his own spiritual poverty. Jesus is not denying his divine status or mission (see 9:37) but is simply calling attention to the fact that before the Father he is total emptiness and receptivity. He is like the child just blessed, for he clings to nothing, receiving all his goodness from God. Jesus then directs the man's attention to the commandments, all of which here concern relations with one's neighbor.

"But I've kept these," counters the man, "from my youth"— that is, from the time of his *bar-mitzvah* at the age of twelve, when he officially took upon himself the whole law. The man is thus spiritually wealthy, but, like the materially wealthy, he wants more and is anxious to *do* whatever is necessary to get it. Jesus feels an impulse of great love for this man, not only for the goodness he has lived but for the desire he has expressed. Nevertheless, he answers his question paradoxically: "You lack because you have too much." Jesus, in effect, asks the man to let go of both his material and his spiritual wealth. His material wealth: "Sell what you have and give to the poor" means just what it says. His spiritual wealth: "Come, follow me" puts the person of Jesus and the joy of being with him above merely observing the law, which had been the man's wealth and security until now. The unexpected invitation is too much, and the man goes away sad, unable to enter the joy of his Lord. When Jesus points out how wealth is an obstacle to the kingdom, his discipls are shocked. They were reared on the Old Testament teaching that wealth is a sign of God's favor (Ps 128:1-2; Job 1:10; 42:10; Is 3:10), and though the poor were also held up as objects of God's concern (Dt 15:7-11; Prv 22:22-23), having wealth meant that one could give more generously to others in alms. But Jesus is categorical. Addressing his disciples affectionately as "children" (and thus calling them to this status before God), he uses the camel-and-needle's-eye image to say that it is impossible for a rich man to enter the kingdom of God. What he means by that is that salvation is entirely God's gift. Attachment to wealth symbolizes man's reliance on his own accomplishments—and these may be spiritual as well as material. Such attachment fundamentally blocks God's offer of his saving gift in the person of Jesus. But with God, in the realization that all is gift from him, everything, including salvation, is possible. Peter, again speaking for all the disciples, joyfully proclaims that they have indeed, unlike the rich man, left everything to follow Jesus. They have forsaken not only wealth but home and family. Jesus responds with his solemn formula, "Amen, I say to you," promising not only eternal life, but even now a spiritual abundance and a family a hundred times as great. This is the spiritual family of which God is father (note the absence of "fathers" in the second half of the promise, v. 30). There will, of course, be persecutions in this life (as Mark's Roman community knows through experience), but even these can be a source of a deeper community bond in Jesus.

The concluding verse 31 is found elsewhere in the gospel tradition in different contexts (Mt 20:16; Lk 13:30), suggesting that many different applications were drawn from it. Here, it may simply confirm the promise just given, or it may, on the other hand, be a caution against the presumption of making their own performance even as disciples (v. 28) a new basis of complacency. From beginning to end, like the kingdom and the person of Jesus, discipleship is gift.

39

His Life a Ransom

10:32-45

³²And they were on the road, going up to Jerusalem and Jesus was walking ahead of them; and they were amazed, and those who followed were afraid. And taking the twelve again, he began to tell them what was to happen to him, ³³saying, "Behold, we are going up to Jerusalem; and the Son of man will be delivered to the chief priests and the scribes, and they will condemn him to death, and deliver him to the Gentiles; ³⁴and they will mock him, and spit upon him, and scourge him, and kill him; and after three days he will rise."

³⁵And James and John, the sons of Zebedee, came forward to him, and said to him, "Teacher, we want you to do for us whatever we ask of you." ³⁶And he said to them, "What do you want me to do for you?" ³⁷And they said to him, "Grant us to sit, one at your right hand and one at your left, in your glory." ³⁸But Jesus said to them, "You do not know what you are asking. Are you able to drink the cup that I drink, or to be baptized with the baptism with which I am baptized?" ³⁹ they said to him, "We are able." And Jesus said to them, "The cup that I drink you will drink; and with the baptism with which I am baptized, you will be baptized; ⁴⁰but to sit at my right hand or at my left is not mine to grant, but it is for those for whom it has been prepared." ⁴¹And when the ten heard it, they began to be indignant at James and John. ⁴²And Jesus called them to him and said to them, "You know that those who are supposed to rule over the Gentiles lord it over them, and their great men exercise authority over them. ⁴³But it shall not be so among you; but

whoever would be great among you must be your servant, [44]and whoever would be first among you must be
slave of all. [45]For the Son of man also came not to be
served but to serve, and to give his life as a ransom for
many."

AGAIN MARK DRAWS our attention to the road, this time men-
tioning Jerusalem explicitly. Jesus walks ahead of his disciples.
This was customary rabbinical practice, but now it is charged
with an awesome and tragic solemnity. Jesus has set his face
toward the holy city. The announcement and fear of the disciples is not caused by their knowing his destination and not
even, it seems, by Jesus' predictions, which they understand
no better this third time than previously. Rather it is Jesus'
solemn determination, his certainty of following a divine mission. It is as if Jesus, who toured Galilee and Samaria and the
surrounding Gentile territory randomly in the first part of his
ministry, is now being led by a mysterious homing device to
the very heart of the nation and the headquarters of his enemies.

Jesus' third prediction contains new elements: He names Jerusalem explicitly, he says the leaders will deliver him to the
Gentiles, the Romans (a most incredible ending for the Messiah!), and he adds details of his passion: "mocked, scourged,
spit upon." He thus predicts the fulfillment of Isaiah 50:6, "I
gave my back to the smiters, and my cheeks to those who
pulled out my beard; I hid not my face from shame and spit-
ting"; and Psalm 22:6-7, "scorned by men, and despised by the
people, all who see me mock at me."

As we pointed out earlier, the structure of 10:32-45 is exactly
parallel with 9:30-37. In each case, Jesus' prediction of his passion is followed by an act of self-interest on the part of the
disciples, revealing their astounding failure to grasp the meaning of the passion, and calling for Jesus' explanation of it in
terms of humility and service.

Here James and John introduce their request, as might children who try to get a commitment from an adult before the

adult knows exactly what is being asked for. Jesus asks them to specify. The two brothers no doubt expect the entry into Jerusalem to be the moment of the final inbreaking of God's kingdom, and they want to reserve for themselves the top positions in the new junta. But they do not know the nature of the kingdom nor the price Jesus is about to pay for it.

"To drink the cup" is obviously to accept and undergo a prepared fate. But biblically the "cup" is most often used of the cup of God's wrath, the cup of his judgment, which God's people in some cases, and her enemies in others, must drink for their sins (Ps 75:8; Jer 25:15-29; Is 51:17-23). Jesus will undergo the lot which others deserve in order to make it possible for them to be spared and healed (Is 53:4-9). The baptism of which Jesus speaks here is equivalent to the "cup." It has the radical sense of submersion and therefore suffering and death. At this point in Mark it ties together the two events of Jesus' baptism in the Jordan and his death on the cross and prepares for Paul's teaching about Christian baptism as a dying with Christ.

James and John, still knowing little of what Jesus' cup is, say they can endure. Jesus predicts they will indeed share his sufferings but that places in the kingdom are not his to give. Jesus, after all, has himself taken the lowest place! The other ten disciples, equally unaware of the crisis of the hour, are indignant at the two. How alone Jesus is on this journey! What confidence he must have that something can be made out of these short-sighted and selfish men he has chosen as pillars for the kingdom! In their rivalries for power they are falling into the value system of the Gentile rulers they despise. Leadership in the community of Jesus means making oneself servant and slave of all. "Servant" is *diakonos*, "deacon" in the Greek, and it refers primarily to one who waits on others at table (Acts 6:2); "slave" has the wider connotation of availability for any kind of service—in this case, not to one or a few in the community but to *all*.

Jesus can make this demand of his disciples because he, the Son of Man, sent by God himself, has not come as triumphant Lord but as lowly servant. Any doubts about whether Jesus is identifying himself with the Lord's servant of Isaiah (Is 52:13-53:12) vanish when we hear his further self-description: "to give his life as a ransom for many." "Many" here does not mean the exclusion of some; it is simply a way of referring to the whole people in contrast to the one servant (Is 53:11). "To give his life" means a voluntary surrender to martyrdom (1 Mc 2:50; 6:44). "Ransom" means the price of deliverance or liberation, as for the release of a captive or slave (Lv 25:51-52; Is 45:13). In the Greek the word translated "for" in "for many" can also mean "in place of," but we must be careful not to take this in a crude sense, as if God were arbitrarily punishing the innocent in order to let the wicked go free. Rather, we must keep in mind the perspective of Isaiah 52-53 (which should be read at this point) and of the whole gospel. Jesus came to deliver his people by preaching and healing. He was rejected, tortured, and executed, but that very act of blind violence on the part of his enemies was for him the supreme expression of his self-giving love. It more than made up in God's eyes for all the wickedness of the world and becomes God's means of deliverance from sin and death for all who accept it. This is what it means to hail Jesus as *redeemer*. This is also what it means to look to him as model of greatness, model of service in the community: "By this we know love, that he laid down his life for us; and we ought to lay down our lives for the brethren" (1 Jn 3:16).

40

"Where You Go, I Will Go"

10:46-52

⁴⁶And they came to Jericho; and as he was leaving Jericho with his disciples and a great multitude, Barti-

maeus, a blind beggar, the son of Timaeus, was sitting by the roadside. [47]And when he heard that it was Jesus of Nazareth, he began to cry out and say, "Jesus, Son of David, have mercy on me!" [48]And many rebuked him, telling him to be silent; but he cried out all the more, "Son of David, have mercy on me!" [49]And Jesus stopped and said, "Call him." And they called the blind man, saying to him, "Take heart; rise, he is calling you." [50]And throwing off his mantle he sprang up and came to Jesus. [51]And Jesus said to him, "What do you want me to do for you?" And the blind man said to him, "Master, let me receive my sight." [52]And Jesus said to him, "Go your way; your faith has made you well. And immediately he received his sight and followed him on the way.

JESUS AND HIS disciples come to Jericho, the town with which Joshua began the conquest of the promised land. At a distance of some eighteen miles from Jerusalem, it was a resting place for pilgrims before the last major portion of their journey. If, as seems likely, Jesus has chosen a major feast as the occasion of his ascent to Jerusalem, the crowds coming with him out of Jericho are mostly pilgrims to the holy city.

In those days no city gate was without its beggars. In a huge crowd, such as the one reported here, a blind beggar would be pushed to the fringe and experience his alienation more than ever. But this particular beggar is different. He will long be remembered in the church, for Mark departs from his usual anonymous description and gives his name, Bartimaeus. Hearing that Jesus is passing by, he cries out, "Jesus, Son of David, have mercy on me." The cry, "have mercy on me," is frequent in the Psalms (4:1; 6:2; 41:4, 10; 51:1). We can be sure that Mark's community sees in this beggar's cry the expression of one of its own acclamations of worship.

The beggar addresses Jesus as Son of David, which in Mark is highly unusual. It is a title of the Messiah, and never before in Mark's gospel has it been used by anyone. In addition, Jesus does not reject or try to silence the confession, as he has done previously to titles of grandeur or messiahship (3:12; 8:30). Later the man simply calls Jesus "Master," but this is also the title Mary Magdalene uses to address the risen Lord in John 20:16.

Even more unusual, however, is the beggar's use of the name *Jesus*. No one up to this point in Mark's gospel has dared use, much less cry out, Jesus' personal name when seeking a cure from him. Here is a daring confession of Jesus' messiahship coupled with an equally daring intimacy in the use of his personal name—a tactic which, undaunted by the repressive attempts of the crowd, goes like an arrow to the heart of Jesus. No wonder Mark's community would remember the personal name of the one who dared to cry out Jesus' personal name!

With vivid detail Mark recounts the interaction between Jesus and Bartimaeus. "Call him," Jesus says. Bartimaeus experiences a thrill of liberation and, apparently unaided, moves to Jesus with that haste of which the blind are somehow capable in crisis moments.

Jesus, of course, knows the man's need, as does everyone else. But he presses the question because it is important to respect the freedom and engage the involvement of the petitioner—a lesson for those who rush to pray for others without asking them what *they* really want to receive. The blind man says the·obvious, but *he* has said it, and that makes the difference.

Unlike the cure of the other blind man (8:22-26) Jesus heals this man instantly. There are other differences as well. In that healing, others brought the blind man and interceded for him. Here, the man himself cries out and approaches Jesus on his own. There, Jesus used spittle and touch; here, only a word. There, Jesus sent the man to his home; here, the man follows Jesus on the way, that is, toward Jerusalem. In both cures, however, there is a teaching about blindness, Jesus' healing, and discipleship. The earlier gradual healing dramatized Jesus' progressive curing of the spiritual blindness of his disciples. The story is located between Jesus' complaint about their blindness (8:14-21) and Peter's lucid confession of Jesus as Messiah

(8:29). Here, the man joyously confesses Jesus as Messiah (Son of David), and, once enlightened by Jesus, follows him *on the way*. This last detail is very significant. Peter, even after confessing Jesus as Messiah, tried to block him from the way of the cross (8:32). Throughout the journey, the disciples fear, doubt, question, and propose petty projects to assure their own advancement. The meaning of the journey escapes them. Bartimaeus, on the contrary, though he may not know the fate awaiting Jesus at the end of his journey, focuses on the only important thing: This man is God's Messiah, and when your life has been totally changed by him, when you can say, "I was blind, but now I see," you want to be with him wherever he goes. A lesson for Mark's community and ours!

41

Hosanna!

11:1-11

11 And when they drew near to Jerusalem, to Bethphage and Bethany, at the Mount of Olives, he sent of his disciples, ²and said to them, "Go into the village opposite you, and immediately as you enter it you will find a colt tied, on which no one has ever sat; untie it and bring it. ³If any one says to you, 'Why are you doing this?' say, 'The Lord has need of it and will send it back here immediately.'" ⁴And they went away, and found a colt tied at the door out in the open street; and they untied it. ⁵And those who stood there said to them, "What are you doing, untying the colt?" ⁶And they told them what Jesus had said; and they let them go. ⁷And they brought the colt to Jesus, and threw their garments on it; and he sat upon it. ⁸And many spread their garments on the road, and others spread leafy branches which they had cut from the fields. ⁹And those who went before and those who followed cried out, "Hosanna! Blessed is he who comes in the name of the Lord! ¹⁰Blessed is the kingdom of our father David that is coming! Hosanna in the highest!"

¹¹And he entered Jerusalem, and went into the temple; and when he had looked round at everything, as it was already late, he went out to Bethany with the twelve.

THE CLIMAX OF Mark's gospel now opens before us: Jesus' final ministry in Jerusalem. The crowds and their festive character suggest that Jesus is accompanied by pilgrims to one of the major festivals. We think at once of Passover. However, since Mark has not shown Jesus in Jerusalem before and yet records (14:49) that he taught daily in the temple (presumably for a considerable period of time), he must have arrived long before the final Passover week of his death. A good guess is that the festival was the preceding fall feast of Tabernacles.

The Mount of Olives rises just to the east of Jerusalem. Bethany was on its eastern slope and Bethphage lay within the precincts of Jerusalem. So the order of Jesus' arrival from the northeast is reversed, probably because Mark wants Jerusalem to dominate the scene. In fact, Bethany was the last pilgrim station. After stopping there, Jesus crossed the Mount of Olives and arrived at Bethphage before entering Jerusalem.

The "village opposite" is probably Bethphage. Was Jesus' word about the colt a clairvoyant "word of knowledge"? Perhaps. On the other hand, it is equally possible that the colt's owner was with Jesus at the time. If so, this would easily explain why the fetching, with the explanation of quick return, brought no objection from the bystanders. "The Lord" here may have meant Jesus or God, but the word can also mean simply "owner."

In any case, Mark sees a profound fulfillment of scripture in the whole scene, beginning with the fact that the colt was tied. In Jacob's prophetic blessing of Judah in Genesis 49:10-11, there is a reference to (1) the one who is coming (the crowds will hail Jesus this way); (2) the obedience of the peoples (the honor given Jesus is a forecast of this); and (3) the colt that is tied to the vine. The fact that the colt has not been broken for common use evokes those Old Testament prescriptions that animals for sacred usages should be unbroken (Nm 19:2; Dt 21:3; 1 Sm 6:7). No doubt Mark also understands this scene to be the fulfillment of Zechariah 9:9, which Matthew cites explicitly: "Shout aloud, O daughter Jerusalem! Lo, your king comes to you . . . humble and riding on an ass, on a colt the foal of an ass."

Caught up in the excitement of the festival and the extraordinary character of the chief pilgrim Jesus, the crowds spontaneously cast their garments before him as when Jehu was hailed as king (2 Kgs 9:13). Others lay branches before him as the crowds hailed Simon when he entered the citadel of Jerusalem (1 Mc 13:51). Was the crowd hailing Jesus as Messiah? Certainly Mark wants his readers to hail Jesus as Messiah and as risen Lord. The careful use, explicit and implicit of Old Testament messianic texts makes this evident. But how deeply this enthusiastic crowd of people perceived all this is not clear. Their cry of "Hosanna! Blessed is he who comes in the name of the Lord!" is taken from Psalm 118:25-26, one of the Hallel psalms that was sung during the feasts of Tabernacles and Passover. This particular verse was originally a blessing upon each pilgrim coming to the feast. At the feast of Tabernacles (the setting we are suggesting), the pilgrims were to carry green fronds and shake them everytime the word "Hosanna" occured. Mark is more reserved in his use of the Hallel text than are Matthew, who has "Son of David," and Luke, who has "King" for the one blessed by the crowd. Mark, who knows well those implications of the scene, is probably closer to the original consciousness of the pilgrim crowd.

Thrilled by reaching its destination and also by having the well-known prophet and wonder-worker along, the crowd bursts into an unplanned chorus of joy that did not involve the whole city in an explicit hailing of Jesus as Messiah—an action which would surely have brought on the immediate intervention of the Roman authorities. Awareness of the different levels of consciousness possible in the this scene—the crowds of pilgrims, the disciples, Jesus, and Mark and his community after the resurrection—makes more understandable the tension in the text between Mark's desire, on the one hand, to make a full-blown confession of who Jesus is and what's *really* happening here (an anticipated Parousia!) and, on the other hand, the restraint imposed on Mark by fidelity to the original historical situation. But even this restraint is part of Mark's message. Can you decode the secret? The Messiah to come on the clouds with hosts of angels comes now on a donkey to the "Hosannas" of a handful of disciples and weary pilgrims.

It has been a long day since leaving Jericho. Jesus goes to inspect the temple as the messenger of the covenant foretold by Malachi (3:1-2), but he will not carry out the purification promised there until the following day.

42

Fig Tree and Temple

11:12-21

[12]On the following day, when they came from Bethany, he was hungry. [13]And seeing in the distance a fig tree in leaf, he went to see if he could find anything on it. When he came to it, he found nothing but leaves, for it was not the season for figs. [14]And he said to it, "May no one ever eat fruit from you again." And his disciples heard it.

[15]And they came to Jerusalem. And he entered the temple and began to drive out those who sold and

those who bought in the temple, and he overturned the tables of the moneychangers and the seats of those who sold pigeons; [16]and he would not allow any one to carry anything through the temple. [17]And he taught, and said to them, "Is it not written, 'My house shall be called a house of prayer for all the nations'? But you have made it a den of robbers." [18]And the chief priests and the scribes heard it and sought a way to destroy him; for they feared him, because all the multitude was astonished at his teaching. [19]And when evening came they went out of the city.

[20]As they passed by in the morning, they saw the fig tree withered away to its roots. [21]And Peter remembered and said to him, "Master, look! The fig tree which you cursed has withered."

JESUS, IN MARK'S gospel, sometimes shocks not only the disciples but also the reader. The cursing of the fig tree is a case in point. At first sight, Jesus appears to act irrationally and spitefully by cursing the fig tree for being barren when it is not the season for figs. Is this, as one scholar called it, "a tale of miraculous power in the service of ill-temper"? If so, Mark would certainly be destroying the crisis-climax of his gospel with the trivial. As usual, the shock alerts the reader to a deeper meaning.

The Old Testament prophets used both vineyard and fig tree as symbols of Israel, called to fruitfulness by her husbandman, the Lord. Jesus will use the vineyard imagery shortly in Mark 12:1-12. The destruction of the fig tree is a frequent symbol of judgment (Is 34:4; Hos 2:2; 9:10, 16; Jl 1:7). The tree's lack of figs while still retaining leaves symbolizes the nation falling short of its calling. "Woe is me!" cries Micah, "For I have become as when the summer fruit has been gathered . . . there is no cluster to eat, no first-ripe fig which my soul desires. The godly man has perished from the earth . . . , they all lie in wait for blood. . . . The day of their watchmen, their punishment has come. . . . Put no confidence in a neighbor, have no confidence in a friend . . . A man's enemies are those of his own house. But as for me, I will look to the Lord, I will wait for the God of my salvation; my God will hear me. Rejoice not over me, O my enemy; when I fall, I shall rise" (Mi 7:1-8). Note how well this passage, begun with the prophet's symbolic hunger for a fig, describes the situation of Jerusalem and the events of Jesus' passion, including his betrayal. In Jeremiah 8:8-13, the Lord condemns the scribes for making the law a lie and the priests for dealing falsely. "Therefore they shall fall among the fallen; when I punish them they shall be overthrown, says the Lord. When I would gather them, says the Lord, there are no grapes on the vine, nor figs on the fig tree; even the leaves are withered."

Jesus' action is thus a prophecy in symbol, like the symbolic actions of the Old Testament prophets. Jeremiah in a similar situation smashed a pot to symbolize Jerusalem's destruction (Jer 19:1-13). Jesus points to the Lord's judgment on the sterility of Jerusalem. The fig tree as a fig tree may have an excuse for barrenness—it's not the season for figs. But the fig tree as Jerusalem has no excuse. God's people must always be ready for his visitation.

Framing as it does the cleansing of the temple (see Mk 11:20-21), the fig tree story is a commentary in action upon the temple and the corruption associated with it. The use of the court of the Gentiles as a trading place for the temple sacrifices was a recent abuse introduced by Caiaphas, the High Priest. There were already four marketplaces approved by the Sanhedrin in the Mount of Olives area. The trading that occurred in the spacious outer pavilion of the temple, where Gentiles favorable to the Jewish religion were allowed to worship, effectively prevented the Gentiles from praying there. Jesus' intervention is not, therefore, an invasion of the inner domain of Jewish worship but a sovereign defense of God's intention to include the Gentiles in the worship that is pleasing to him. In Jesus' citation of Isaiah 56:7, the emphasis falls on *all the nations*. The prophet Malachi had not only prophesied the coming of this mighty purifier of temple and priesthood (Mal 3:1-4) but had also said that the sacrifices of good Gentiles were more pleasing to God than the corrupt sacrifices of the Jerusalem priests (Mal 1:6-14). Mark's community in Rome, a mixture of

Jewish and non-Jewish Christians, could well appreciate this action in which Jesus welcomes the worship of the Gentiles.

Money-changers were also present to enable Jews to convert their Roman coins into the Tyrian shekel used to pay the annual temple tax. Pigeons or doves were available for the poor who could not afford the more costly offerings (Lv 12:6; Lk 2:22-24). However, none of this activity is acceptable to Jesus in this place of prayer. Not only does he restore the demand of Zechariah 14:21 that no trader be in the temple, he even forbids anyone to use the Gentile court as a "short-cut" for secular traffic. All this activity, says Jesus, amounts to making the temple a den of robbers—an expression borrowed from the temple speech of Jeremiah (7:11) and evoking the prophecy of destruction uttered there.

The chief priests and the scribes seek to destroy Jesus, even though his action here was actually a rigorous interpretation of the scribal law! The people's astonishment at his teaching may indicate that Jesus spent more time doing this than is reported or that his teaching is different because it was done with authority (see 1:27).

Again Jesus leaves the city. The next morning the disciples discover the fig tree withered. This provides the interpretation of the temple cleansing and predicts the judgment to come upon Jerusalem. We turn next to another lesson to be drawn from the withering of the fig tree.

43

Of Faith and Authority
11:22-33

²²And Jesus answered them, "Have faith in God. ²³Truly, I say to you, whoever says to this mountain, 'Be taken up and cast into the sea,' and does not doubt

in his heart, but believes that what he says will come to pass, it will be done for him." [24]Therefore I tell you, whatever you ask in prayer, believe that you receive it, and you will. [25]And whenever you stand praying, forgive, if you have anything against any one; so that your Father also who is in heaven may forgive you your trespasses."

[27]And they came again to Jerusalem. And as he was walking in the temple, the chief priests and the scribes and the elders came to him, [28]and they said to him, "By what authority are you doing these things, or who gave you this authority to do them?" [29]Jesus said to them, "I will ask you a question; answer me, and I will tell you by what authority I do these things. [30]Was the baptism of John from heaven or from men? Answer me." [31]And they argued with one another, "If we say, 'From heaven,' he will say, 'Why then did you not believe him?' [32]But shall we say, 'From men'?"—they were afraid of the people, for all held that John was a real prophet. [33]So they answered Jesus, "We do not know." And Jesus said to them, "Neither will I tell you by what authority I do these things."

WHILE THE WITHERING of the fig tree is primarily a prophetic action about Jerusalem, it also provides the occasion to teach about prayer for difficult things. Even if Mark has assembled sayings of Jesus from other situations, they fit into a beautiful teaching on two essential points for Christian prayer: faith and forgiveness.

The mountain may, of course, be just a metaphor for difficult things. Paul seems to take it that way when he speaks about the faith that moves mountains (1 Cor 13:2). On the other hand, it might signify the temple mount which will be replaced by Jesus himself and those who believe in him. Or, it might imply the Mount of Olives itself. Zechariah had prophesied that on the day of the Lord's coming the Mount of Olives would be split in two (Zec 14:4-5). Isaiah also had prophesied the leveling of mountains (Is 40:4). The prayer here, then, may well refer to the prayer in faith for the coming of the kingdom.

However, the emphasis is on faith and confidence that what we ask for will be given us. This could, of course, lead to introspective anxiety, concentrating more on the faith of the petitioner than on the fidelity of the giver. The confidence that what we ask for has already been given is founded by Paul in the all-encompassing gift we have received in Jesus. If the Father has given us all in Jesus, could he refuse us anything less (Rom 8:32)? Thus the prayer of faith is simultaneously intercession and thanksgiving for the same request.

Finally, this power of intercession presumes forgiveness. God will not release his power if the one praying will not set free anyone he holds in bonds of unforgiveness.

Verse 26 is dropped from most modern translations because it is not in the best Greek manuscripts. Some scribes simply copied Matthew's additional words here, "But if you do not forgive, neither will your Father who is in heaven, forgive your trespasses" (Mt 6:15).

Again in Jerusalem, Jesus is walking in one of the temple porches and is approached by a delegation of chief priests, scribes, and elders—probably official representatives of the Sanhedrin. Notice how throughout his ministry opposition to Jesus comes not from the people but from their leaders. They demand to know where he claimed to get the authority to cleanse the temple. Was it his own authority, and thus does he claim to be a prophet directly inspired by God? Or is he the delegate or instrument of some other authority?

In rabbinical debate, cleverness in silencing the opponent was often more highly regarded than logic. In this case Jesus uses both by the common rabbinical technique of answering questions with a question. He puts them on the horns of a practical dilemma in which either answer would disgrace them before the people, who are obviously listening in the background. Jesus and John are one in their preaching of reform for the sake of the kingdom. In the eyes of the people, then, what they say of John holds equally well for Jesus. To avoid the trap they answer, "We do not know"—an embarrassing statement from those who are supposed to be able to discern true and false prophets; but under the circumstances it is the only way out of the dilemma. Jesus, in turn, refuses to reveal the source of his authority.

From this scene it is obvious that Jesus himself has made no public claim to be the Messiah, or even a prophet. If he had, there would have been no need to question him about authority. This is a very important point for Mark. Even with his disciples Jesus is reserved about his identity. When Peter identifies him as the Messiah, Jesus does not, in Mark, openly accept this title and praise Peter for the confession. Rather he calls attention to his role as suffering servant. Jesus' identity remains a mystery to be fully revealed only on the cross.

44

Tenants and Cornerstone

12:1-12

12 And he began to speak to them in parables. "A man planted a vineyard, and set a hedge around it, and dug a pit for the wine press, and built a tower, and let it out to tenants, and went into another country. ²When the time came, he sent a servant to the tenants, to get from them some of the fruit of the vineyard. ³And they took him and beat him, and sent him away empty-handed. ⁴Again he sent to them another servant, and they wounded him in the head, and treated him shamefully. ⁵And he sent another, and him they killed; and so with many others, some they beat and some they killed. ⁶He had still one other, a beloved son; finally he sent him to them, saying, 'They will respect my son.' ⁷But those tenants said to one another, 'This is the heir; come, let us kill him, and the inheritance will be ours.' [8]And they took him and killed him, and cast him out of the vineyard, [9]What will the owner of the vineyard do? He will come and destroy the tenants, and give the vineyard to others. [10]Have you not read this scripture:

'The very stone which the builders rejected
has become the head of the corner;
[11]this was the Lord's doing,
and it is marvelous in our eyes'?"
[12]And they tried to arrest him, but feared the multitude, for they perceived that he had told the parable against them; so they left him and went away.

THE DELEGATION OF priests, scribes, and elders who came to Jesus with the question about authority are still present as Jesus tells this parable. It is not an allegory in which every detail can be pressed for symbolic meaning. It is a parable, a story with one point, even though some of its details may also be symbolic. Jesus tells them the story of a man who planted a vineyard and went through the elaborate preparation necessary to protect it and to harvest its fruits and produce wine. Any Jewish listener would think immediately of Isaiah 5:1-4: "My beloved had a vineyard on a very fertile hill. He digged it and cleared it of stones, and planted it with choice vines; he built a watchtower in the midst of it and hewed out a wine vat in it; and he looked for it to yield grapes, but it yielded wild grapes." The Isaiah text goes on to describe the owner's coming judgment upon his vineyard, which verse 7 identifies as the house of Israel.

The difference in Jesus' use of this text is that the problem lies not with the vineyard but with the tenants who are put in charge of it. Obviously, Jesus is not directing this parable at the Jewish people but at the leaders who are listening, and they understand it this way as well (v. 12).

In the Galilee of Jesus' day, absentee landlords were quite

common. They would occasionally send inspectors and, particularly at harvest time, expect the owner's share of the "fruit of the vineyard," that is, a shipment of wine. There is evidence, however, of considerable unrest among the tenant farmers at this period, and problems similar to the one described here were not uncommon. In this case, the tenants beat the first servant, wound and abuse the second. The owner continues to send servants, some of whom they beat and some of whom they kill. At this point the parable intentionally exaggerates, revealing its deeper meaning. No human owner would put up with such conduct. But if the servants are the prophets, and they are often called "servants" in the Bible (Am 3:7; Jer 7:25; 25:4; Zec 1:6), it is clear that we are confronted with an owner whose patience and long-suffering are really divine: The owner is the Lord.

So bent is he on obtaining his due from the vineyard that he finally sends his son, who is his "beloved." This could mean "only son" (see Gn 22:2). The note of affection is certainly there, but even more so the idea that this is the very last mission. There will be no other. It is part of the divine irony of the story that God acts in such a foolhardy way, willing to send his own son and unwilling to believe that the tenants are so badly disposed that they will kill even his son.

The tenants, however, seeing the son coming, assume the owner is dead. Only this assumption, though false, lends sense to their hopes that the land will lie without an owner if they kill the son, in which case they could seize it. So they kill him and throw his body over the vineyard wall.

Jesus then addresses the question of what the owner will do. "Giving the vineyard to others" need not be a detail with symbolism, although if it is, the "others" are probably not the Gentiles but the new leaders—the Twelve.

Then he quotes from Psalm 118, the Hallel psalm from which the crowds sang as Jesus entered the city. Verses 22 and 23 immediately precede the hosanna chorus. Already in the Old Testament the verse was a parable for the just man who, despite rejection by the mighty, is upheld and vindicated by God. It was understood to apply to David, the least of Jesse's sons, who was chosen as king to unite the people. It was later applied to the reigning king, who participated in the liturgy of the feast. When Israel was deprived of a king, it was applied to the descendent of David, the king-Messiah to come. Hence Jesus is coming ever closer to a public revelation of his identity. The builders are the leaders listening to his words, the temple authorities of 11:27. They will reject Jesus, but God will set him as the cornerstone of a new people, replacing the temple.

45

What Belongs to God

12:13-27

[13]And they sent to him some of the Pharisees and some of the Herodians, to entrap him in his talk. [14]And they came and said to him, "Teacher, we know that you are true, and care for no man; for you do not regard the position of men, but truly teach the way of God. Is it lawful to pay taxes to Caesar, or not? [15]Should we pay them, or should we not?" But knowing their hypocrisy, he said to them, "Why put me to the test? Bring me a coin, and let me look at it. [16]And they brought one. And he said to them, "Whose likeness and inscription is this?" They said to him, "Caesar's." [17]Jesus said to them, "Render to Caesar the things that are Caesar's, and to God the things that are God's." And they were amazed at him.

[18]And Sadducees came to him, who say that there is no resurrection; and they asked him a question, saying, [19]"Teacher, Moses wrote for us that if a man's brother dies and leaves a wife, but leaves no child, the man must take the wife, and raise up children for his

brother. [20]There were seven brothers; the first took a wife, and when he died left no children; [21]and the second took her, and died, leaving no children; and the third likewise; [22]and the seven left no children. Last of all the woman also died. [23]In the resurrection whose wife will she be? For the seven had her as wife."

[24]Jesus said to them, "Is not this why you are wrong, that you know neither the scriptures, nor the power of God? [25]For when they rise from the dead, they neither marry nor are given in marriage, but are like angels in heaven. [26]And as for the dead being raised, have you not read in the book of Moses, in the passage about the bush, how God said to him, 'I am the God of Abraham, and the God of Isaac, and the God of Jacob'? [27]He is not God of the dead, but of the living; you are quite wrong."

EARLY IN HIS Galilean ministry Jesus came into conflict with the established teachers and observers of the law. The five conflicts that took place there (Mk 2:1-3:5) climaxed in the plot of the Pharisees and the Herodians to destroy him (3:6). Now, in Jerusalem, another series of conflicts sets the stage for the culmination of this plot in the passion and death of Jesus. The first of these conflicts was evoked by the parable of the wicked tenants; the second, reported here, is the dispute over paying tribute to Caesar. The Pharisees and Herodians, whose plotting has been reported in Galilee (12:13; 3:6), first extol Jesus' virtue and fearless truthfulness and then try to trap him with their question.

The question they pose is a "hot potato." The Roman census taken around the time of Jesus' infancy had led to a system of taxation called the tribute. The hot-blooded zealots refused to pay the tax, the Pharisees resented the tax but paid it, and the Herodians supported the tax as part of their overall policy of collaboration with Rome. Jesus is asked if his interpretation of the law of God permits paying the tax or not. By answering "yes" he would alienate the zealots and the people in general;

by answering "no" he would invite the intervention of the Roman authorities. The insincerity of the question is exposed by the fact that though the Pharisees and the Herodians usually opposed each other they have momentarily agreed to work together to dispose of Jesus.

Jesus sees through the trick. It is the playing out of the tempter's role, first modeled by Satan (1:13). Instead of immediately answering, he calls for a denarius. Not only is this strategy a masterful way to dramatize a teaching; it introduces a further dimension of the question, since the image of Caesar was accompanied by the words "Son of the divine Augustus," a claim to divine honors.

Jesus' response, "Render to Caesar what is Caesar's and to God what is God's," resolves the dilemma by taking it to a deeper level. Several things are implied in his answer: First, the civil government has a certain autonomy and rights. Jesus does not consider civil government an evil soon to be abolished by the inbreaking of God's rule. The zealots find no support here for their revolutionary stand, even though the Romans may have taken the land by violence. Second, however, there is no whitewashing of imperial Rome either, for emperor worship is idolotry, and the temptation of the State is always to assume more power than rightfully belongs to it.

Jesus does not specify what exactly belongs to Caesar and what belongs to God, but he does acknowledge the legitimate rights of both. All of Christian history could be written in the light of the meaning of this phrase.

Jesus' enemies are not merely silenced. They are amazed at the brilliance of his answer, even as they plot to destroy him.

The third dispute is with the Sadducees, who deny the reality of life after death. They base their teaching on their claim that the Law, that is, the first five books of the Bible, teaches nothing about the resurrection and that the later appearance of the doctrine was a deviation from the authentic word of God. They argue from the provision Moses made for the continuance of the family name when a man dies leaving no children (Dt 25:5). They propose the extreme case of a woman who had seven successive husbands. In the supposed life of the resurrection, which they assume will restore all human relationships, whose wife would she be? This question also is a trick, but Jesus is not unprepared. His questioners know neither the scriptures nor the power of God.

Though the resurrection is bodily, it is also a transformation into angelic glory in which union with God is the primary relationship and earthly relationships are entirely secondary. Marriage is characteristic of the earthly life. In Ephesians 5:25-32 it is a symbol of the union of Christ with his church; when the reality is consummated, the symbol disappears.

The Sadducees are also ignorant of the scriptures. Jesus draws his argument from the book considered authoritative by the Sadducees. He does not seek to prove the resurrection as a logical consequence of a human being's having a spiritual soul. Rather he looks to God's covenant fidelity. When God spoke to Moses out of the burning bush, he grounded his promise of salvation on the fact that he was "the God of Abraham, the God of Isaac, the God of Jacob" (Ex 3:16). God's promise to give them land and posterity is being fulfilled in what he is now doing. If God is the author of covenant relationship, then death cannot be the termination of that relationship, especially if God's promise has not yet been fulfilled. For he is the living God, and if he is the God *of* someone, then that someone shares in the living power of the God to whom he belongs.

This is the very root of the New Testament understanding of the resurrection. If God makes a covenant and swears his fidelity, not even death itself can block his fulfillment of that promise. Or, as the book of Wisdom says, "Righteousness (i.e. God's covenant union) is immortal" (Wis 1:15) and "To know your power is the root of immortality" (Wis 15:3). The error of the Sadducees was that, in practice, they denied the power and the fidelity of Israel's covenant God.

Thus the dispute over the resurrection is related to the preceding dispute over the coin of tribute. When God raises the just to life, it is simply his way of claiming what belongs to him.

Greatest Law and Greatest Son

12:28-37

²⁸And one of the scribes came up and heard them disputing with one another, and seeing that he answered them well, asked him, "Which commandment is the first of all?" ²⁹Jesus answered, "The first is, 'Hear, O Israel: The Lord our God, the Lord is one; ³⁰and you shall love the Lord your God with all your heart, and with all your soul, and with all your mind, and with all your strength.' ³¹The second is this, 'You shall love your neighbor as yourself.' There is no other commandment greater than these." ³²And the scribe said to him, "You are right, Teacher; you have truly said that he is one, and there is no other but he; ³³and to love him with all the heart, and with all the understanding, and with all the strength, and to love one's neighbor as oneself,' is much more than all whole burnt offerings and sacrifices." ³⁴And when Jesus saw that he answered wisely, he said to him, "You are not far from the kingdom of God." And after that no one dared to ask him any question.

³⁵And as Jesus taught in the temple, he said, "How can the scribes say that the Christ is the son of David? ³⁶David himself, inspired by the Holy Spirit, declared,

'The Lord said to my Lord,
Sit at my right hand,
till I put thy enemies under thy feet.'
³⁷David himself calls him Lord; so how is he his son?" And the great throng heard him gladly.

THE SCRIBE'S QUESTION here seems more honestly motivated than the preceding ones. He notices how well Jesus has responded to the previous question, and he brings to the Teacher a question that has probably more significance for him than an intellectual curiosity. Amid the hundreds of laws in the Bible, which is the first, the most foundational? What law puts the rest in proper perspective?

Jesus responds by quoting the *Shema*, the Jews' daily prayer. The command to love the Lord with one's whole being is rooted in the fact that the Lord is one. There is only one God, the Lord, and he is not even many gods under one form. Hence, there is no basis for divided loyalties, especially in view of the fact that the Lord has chosen and covenanted himself with this people. He claims their total allegiance. "Heart, soul, mind, strength," are simply Jewish ways of expressing a consecration of one's whole being to the Lord.

The scribe asked only about the *first* commandment, but in his answer Jesus includes what he considers the second—to love one's neighbor as oneself. This is not part of the *Shema*. It indicates that for Jesus the love of neighbor is inseparable from the love of God. "There is no greater commandment than *these*"—that is, to answer the question of the greatest commandment only by the love of God is to overlook an essential implication of one's love of God, the neighbor. "Neighbor" in Leviticus 29:18 meant, of course, a member of the Jewish people. In the parable of the Good Samaritan all such limitations are swept away (Lk 10:25-37). This basic teaching of Jesus on the love of neighbor becomes a foundation stone of New Testament ethics (Gal 5:14; Rom 13:8-9; Jas 2:8; 1 Jn 3:11-18).

The scribe is surprisingly expansive in his response to Jesus' answer. He adds that this love defined by Jesus is greater than giving God the most perfect Old Testament offering, the holocaust. Already the Old Testament had taught that obedience and praise were superior to sacrifice (1 Sm 15:22; Ps 51:15-17), and the same was true of faithful love (Hos 6:6). By placing the love of God and neighbor above all the commandments and sacrifices, the scribe suggests that love has a certain sacrificial and atoning character about it. Indeed, as the return of one's whole being to God (v. 30), it is the sacrifice most pleasing to God.

Jesus tells the scribe, "You are not far from the kingdom of God." Deuteronomy 30:14 already said, "The word [of God's law] is very near you, it is in your mouth and in your heart for your observance." The scribe has demonstrated this and has shown his readiness for the kingdom. He does not ask what more is needed, as did the good rich man of 10:17-27, but we can surmise that the decision to follow Jesus is all that he lacks.

Since Jesus wins admirers even among those who try him with questions, his enemies decide not to ask him any more questions. So Jesus himself takes the initiative and poses the question about David's son. Several assumptions underlie his question. It was common scribal teaching that the Messiah would be descended from David. This was based on many Old Testament texts (such as Is 9:2-7; 11:1-9; Jer 23:5-6; Ez 34:23-24; Hos 3:5) but especially on those psalms that were chanted during the enthronement of each new king of the Davidic dynasty. One of these psalms was Psalm 110, in which the poet said, "The Lord [God] said to my lord [the king], 'Sit at my right hand, till I make your enemies a footstool for your feet.'" It was the Lord's promise of victory for the king being enthroned. Later, when the people were without a king, this psalm was still used, but as a promise of the King-Messiah to come. Also, since David was the great Old Testament psalmist, he was understood to have said this psalm himself concerning the coming Messiah. But in that case, Jesus asks, how could David give the Messiah the title "Lord" if he is only David's son? Implied in Jesus' question, the climax of his disputes, is that the Messiah must be more than merely the Son of David. Jesus does not proclaim himself to be that Messiah here, but the Christian reader knows who he is, proclaimed such by Peter (8:29) and soon to be proclaimed Son of God as well (15:39).

The common people continue to listen eagerly, and the opposition between Jesus and the scribes mounts.

47

She Gave Everything

12:38-44

³⁸And in his teaching he said, "Beware of the scribes, who like to go about in long robes, and to have salutations in the market places ³⁹and the best seats in the synagogues and the places of honor at feasts, ⁴⁰who devour widows' houses and for a pretense make long prayers. They will receive the greater condemnation."

⁴¹And he sat down opposite the treasury, and watched the multitude putting money into the treasury. Many rich people put in large sums. ⁴²And a poor widow came, and put in two copper coins, which make a penny. ⁴³And he called his disciples to him, and said to them, "Truly, I say to you, this poor widow has put in more than all those who are contributing to the treasury. ⁴⁴For they all contributed out of their abundance; but she out of her poverty has put in everything she had, her whole living."

THROUGHOUT THE GOSPEL, the scribes have unsuccessfully used the tactic of legal debate to trap Jesus. He has won on every score. Now, after having moved to the offensive concerning their teaching, Jesus openly attacks their example.

The scribes were the experts in the law. Some translations call them "lawyers," but inasmuch as the law was the basis not just for civil or criminal justice but for all of Jewish life, especially its religious life, the scribes really functioned as theologians. They were scholars whose authority derived from their knowledge of the law. The Sadducees as well as the Pharisees had their scribes, who argued from the law to support their various beliefs. Because of their position they came to enjoy great respect, even being seated in the synogogue facing the congregation. It was customary for common folk to rise and greet the scribes, and at dinner they were given the places of highest honor. They wore a large white stole called a *tallith* and were easily distinguishable from others who generally wore colored clothing.

While passages like this paint a dark picture of the scribes, other sources and even certain passages of Mark (12:28-34) show many of them as sincerely motivated. The problem is the abuse of their status into which many of them fell, not only in fostering marks of prestige but even in "devouring the houses of widows"—that is, living on fees or donations from those in Jewish society least able to afford them. Jesus warns the crowds and especially his disciples to avoid such conduct. Religious leaders who abuse their status will receive a judgment heavier than the sinner whom the scribes condemn (see 2:16).

The final scene is a precious one, climactic for Jesus' own teaching in the temple. In the outer temple area there were collection boxes at thirteen stations around the court of the women. Jesus' busy preaching activity has not dimmed his keen eye. He sees a poor widow making her way to the collection box, after a number of wealthy donors who have made little effort to conceal the size of their offerings. The woman has but two of the smallest coins in circulation. The old English translation called them "mites." In American coinage they would be pennies. In Roman times it took two of them to make a *quadrans*.

The disciples would have been impressed, no doubt, at the large contributions being made by the wealthy, measuring virtue by quantity. Jesus has a lesson for them. The heroine of the story is the poor widow who gave her *all*. Let the disciples raise what objections they might about the folly of a poor woman giving away her whole subsistence. That is precisely the point. For at this particular moment in Jesus' life, standing as he is in the courtyard of that holy place where man gives himself to God and God to man, the woman typifies the folly Jesus himself is about to commit—to give his *all* for the ransom of many (10:45). Small wonder that Jesus' attention would be drawn to her. Small wonder too that Mark would preserve this story as a lesson for the disciples who should follow Jesus to the cross rather than follow the scribes to the seats of honor. Unlike those who devour the houses of widows (12:40), the disciple Jesus admires will, like the poor widow, give all, though he may not be noticed by anyone but the Lord. It is just such "little" people like the poor obscure widow who make the headlines God reads.

48

Jesus and the Future

Chapter 13

WE NOW COME to Mark's chapter 13, which has been called Jesus' apocalyptic discourse. Its language and style are different from the rest of the gospel, and there has been much dispute about what is being taught here. Before exploring each part in detail, it is necessary to deal with some general questions about the chapter as a whole.

A good way to discover the meaning of this long section is to ask the question, what would Mark's gospel be like without it? Without it, we would wonder what is the relationship between Jesus' public ministry, and especially the tragic ending of his life, to his original heralding, "the kingdom of God is at hand" (1:15). Jesus preached that the kingdom was imminent, and he gave signs that it was beginning to break in even now through the healings and exorcisms of his ministry. But was his death and the empty tomb God's last word about the kingdom? The answer of chapter 13 is "no!" God will continue to unfold his kingdom through historical events such as the destruction of the temple, and he will close history with the glorious coming of the Son of Man—both related to the first coming of Jesus, his passion and death (see 14:62). Without chapter 13, we would also be puzzled at the references in the passion story to the destruction of the temple (see 14:58). What did Jesus really teach about the temple? Finally, without chapter 13, an important part of Jesus' teaching about the persecution of the disciples would be missing. Mark's community in Rome is experiencing just that. Mark has already recorded what Jesus said during his public ministry about the cost of following him (8:34-38). But in chapter 13 Jesus predicts what will beset the disciples when he is no longer physically present. He tells the community how to live in the midst of political and cosmic upheavals. They are not to be misled into thinking that these are signs that the end is at hand. They are to especially beware the seduction of false messiahs.

This chapter, then, provides a cosmic screen on which to view the coming events of Jesus' passion, death, and resurrection. This purpose also explains the new shape that the discourse takes. It is a mixture of apocalyptic forecast and farewell discourse. *Apocalyptic* is a kind of literature that became popular in Judaism in the last two centuries before Christ. Born in the seed-bed of persecution, it is literature that deals with present and future in coded images, often using the raw materials of past biblical stories to describe present or future characters or events. For example, the book of Daniel relates stories about Nebuchadnezzer, the ruthless Babylonian king who destroyed Jerusalem and enslaved the Jews; but the reader of Daniel knows that the author is *really* talking about the Greek king Antiochus the Illustrious, who is persecuting the Jews at the time the book was written. This method of teaching about contemporary events shows how God's history with his people *now* is like it was *then*. It also avoids the danger of being easily identified by the persecutor should the document fall into his hands. Jesus will use much biblical imagery of the past to describe the events that will befall his disciples. It is as if he were saying, "The same kind of things will happen in your lifetime that happened in the biblical stories you are familiar with."

However, apocalyptic writers often traced their picture of the future to a special vision they or their heroes received. It is not so with Jesus. The reason is that, while using some apocalyptic imagery, his words here are also—and even more importantly—a farewell discourse.

Other great biblical figures, as they saw death approaching, gathered their children or disciples for a final testament and exhortation: Jacob (Gn 49:21-49), Moses (Dt 31-32), Joshua (Jos 23-24), Samuel (1 Sm 12), David (1 Chr 28-29). Paul does the same in Acts 20:17-38. As for Jesus, we are more familiar perhaps with the Last Supper discourse in John 14-17. But in the three other gospels, the lengthy final teaching of Jesus appears *before* the Last Supper, in the form of a final teaching delivered in or about Jerusalem, the temple, and the future, up to the glorious coming of the Son of Man. The net result is a strong exhortation to fidelity and perseverance. It is also a warning against the fanaticism so easily turned to by disciples who would see troubled times as the sure mark of the end of the world and the second coming.

49

The End Is Not Yet

13:1-13

13 And as he came out of the temple, one of his disciples said to him, "Look, Teacher, what wonderful stones and what wonderful buildings!" ²And Jesus said to him, "Do you see these great buildings? There will not be left here one stone upon another, that will not be thrown down."

³And as he sat on the Mount of Olives opposite the temple, Peter and James and John and Andrew asked him privately, ⁴"Tell us, when will this be, and what will be the sign when these things are all to be accom-

plished?" ⁵And Jesus began to say to them, "Take heed that no one leads you astray. ⁶Many will come in my name, saying, 'I am he!' and they will lead many astray. ⁷And when you hear of wars and rumors of wars, do not be alarmed; this must take place, but the end is not yet. ⁸For nation will rise against nation, and kingdom against kingdom; there will be earthquakes in various places, there will be famines; this is but the beginning of the sufferings.

⁹"But take heed to yourselves; for they will deliver you up to councils; and you will be beaten in synagogues; and you will stand before governors and kings for my sake, to bear testimony before them. ¹⁰And the gospel must first be preached to all nations. ¹¹And when they bring you to trial and deliver you up, do not be anxious beforehand what you are to say; but say whatever is given you in that hour, for it is not you who speak, but the Holy Spirit. ¹²And brother will deliver up brother to death, and the father his child, and children will rise against parents and have them put to death; ¹³and you will be hated by all for my name's sake. But he who endures to the end will be saved.

EVEN TODAY A visitor looking upon the vast temple area in Jerusalem and some of the foundation stones at the wailing wall experiences amazement. How much more impressive was it in Jesus' day when the temple rebuilt by Herod commanded the view! Thus Jesus' prophecy of the temple's destruction comes as a shock. As the disciples reach the Mount of Olives and enjoy the splendid panorama of city and temple, the three intimate disciples and Andrew question Jesus privately. The form of their question is very important to understanding the whole discourse, which is meant to be Jesus' answer.

The question has two parts: (1) *When* will *this* (singular) happen? and (2) What will be the *sign* that all these *things* (plural) are to be accomplished? In all likelihood the two parts are simply the characteristic Semitic way of asking one question in parallel forms. However, the use of the plural in the second form means that the disciples think of the destruction of the temple as necessarily closing an age of history, as part of a cosmic collapse of some kind. As Jews, they held that the temple was one of the foundations of the world. Using language like that of Daniel 12:6-7 in a similar situation, they ask Jesus for some *sign* that this end-event is about to happen.

In his response, Jesus weaves together a series of biblical phrases to tell his disciples what things will *not* be signs of the end. "Take heed" is a phrase used four times in this discourse (vv. 5, 9, 23, 33). It indicates that Jesus' focus is not upon a crystal-ball revelation of the future but rather upon what discipleship will mean in the midst of a chaotic and confusing future, when it may seem that the end will never come. In such crises, disciples will long for the return of Jesus. But precisely that longing may make them vulnerable to those who would claim either to be Jesus returning or to be sent by him ("in my name"). They may even claim Jesus' own divine title and status ("I am he"). In first-century Palestine, several messianic pretenders did arise and, capturing the momentary hopes of zealous Jews, led them to destruction.

Nor are wars, earthquakes, and famines to be read as signs of the immediate end. The emphasis in verses 7-8 is on the phrases "but the end is not yet" and "this is but the beginning of the birthpangs." Jesus is saying, "Do not expect immediate relief. Be willing to endure these and much more." "Birthpangs" is a contemporary image of the sufferings the people would have to endure before the coming of the Messiah. Even such cosmic things as wars, earthquakes, and famines are signs not of the end but only of the beginning.

This is a teaching of Jesus that future generations of Christians have not always heeded. "End-time" prophets have periodically appeared reading such cosmic events as signs of the imminent end, contrary to the teaching here.

Neither are the disciples to be surprised at their own persecution by Jewish or Gentile authorities. "Councils (literally, sanhedrins) and synagogues" refer to Jewish institutions, "governors and kings" may include Gentiles, though all of this could happen in Palestine as well as Rome.

With the exception of verse 10, the rest of this section is simply counsel and reassurance in persecution. When the Christian experiences the same lot as Jesus, namely being "delivéred up" (3:19; 9:31; 10:33; 14:11, 18, 21, 41; 15:1, 10, 15), he should realize that this vocation entitles him to the support of Jesus' own Spirit, who will lead the witnessing and inspire the words. One thinks of Joan of Arc who, when asked by her judges the tricky question, "Are you in the state of grace?" responded, "If I am, I pray the Lord keep me there; if I am not, I pray he put me there."

Loyalty to Jesus may not only cause the rupture of family ties but the tragedy of betrayal by one's own family.

Verse 10 is another clear delay-teaching, inserted here probably because it connects with the witnessing spoken of in verses 9 and 11. "First" means that the end will not come before the good news about Jesus is preached to all the Gentiles—which could, of course, mean all the nations of the earth, or, symbolically, all the nations represented by Rome, capital of the then-known world. As a matter of fact, the temple was not destroyed before the gospel was preached in Rome.

Finally, the teaching of this whole section climaxes in its exhortation to persevere *to the end*—that is, even to death if necessary. Jesus offers no promise to his disciples that he will intervene to spare them his own martyr's destiny. There is glory, but it is certain only on the other side of the cross, even for the disciple.

50

"Flee For Your Lives!"

13:14-23

¹⁴"But when you see the desolating sacrilege set up where it ought not to be (let the reader understand), then let those who are in Judea flee to the mountains; ¹⁵let him who is on the housetop not go down, nor enter his house, to take anything away; ¹⁶and let him who is in the field not turn back to take his mantle. ¹⁷And alas for those who are with child and for those who give suck in those days! ¹⁸Pray that it may not happen in winter. ¹⁹For in those days there will be such tribulation as has not been from the beginning of the creation which God created until now, and never will be. ²⁰And if the Lord had not shortened the days, no human being would be saved; but for the sake of the elect, whom he chose, he shortened the days. ²¹And then if any one says to you, 'Look, here is the Christ!' or 'Look, there he is!' do not believe it. ²²False Christs and false prophets will arise and show signs and wonders, to lead astray, if possible, the elect. ²³But take heed; I have told you all things beforehand.

IF JESUS REFUSES to tell his disciples when the end will occur and warns them against looking for signs of relief from cosmic upheavals and persecutions, he does have some specific directions as to what to do when the destruction of Jerusalem approaches.

The "desolating sacrilege" ("abomination of desolation" in some translations) is an expression taken from the Book of Daniel (9:27; 11:31; 12:11) and identified in 1 Maccabees 1:54 as the altar to Zeus which the Greek King Antiochus IV erected over the altar of holocausts in the temple. He offered swine's flesh on it and put to death anyone who was caught observing the Jewish religion. Here in Mark it becomes one of those past biblical events used to describe a present or future event. Significantly, the neuter "sacrilege" is followed by the masculine "he" and should be translated: "the desolating sacrilege standing where *he* ought not to be." Mark cues his reader: "you should know *who* this is." To whom does this refer? One thinks, of course, of Titus and his Roman legions who marched on Jerusalem to crush the Jewish revolt in 66-70 A.D. The prophecy suggests, however, that something would happen *in the temple* as a sign preceding the impending disaster. Some scholars therefore point to the desecrating activity engaged in there by (of all people!) the Jewish zealots whose political ambition overcame their piety as they took control of the revolt. In 67-68 A.D. they actually went through the farce of installing one Phanni, a clown, as high priest. About this time too, the zealots began to hinder those who sought to leave the city. It would make perfect sense, then, that the Jewish Christians who until then had continued to visit the temple as part of their worship (cf. Acts 2:46) should take this installation of Phanni as a signal to hasten from the city.

As a matter of fact, the early church historian Eusebius tells us that the Christians living in Jerusalem were warned by prophecy of the coming destruction and fled to Pella across the Jordan. The brutal description given by the Jewish historian Josephus of the siege and the conquest of Jerusalem confirms how fully Jesus' awful prophecy was fulfilled (see Josephus' book, *The Jewish Wars*).

Jesus counsels haste. If one is at prayer on the roof of his house, he must leave by the outside ladder and not reenter his house. If one is working the field and has left his coat at another place, he must not go back for it. As always happens in times of great disaster, pregnant or nursing women will suffer most. Winter is a particularly hard time for flight, not only because of the cold, but because the winter rains may swell the dry creek-beds, blocking passage.

The first part of verse 19 is an almost literal quotation of

Daniel 12:1: "It shall be a time unsurpassed in distress since nations began until that time." The final words, "and never will be," indicate that the suffering spoken of here is that connected with the destruction of Jerusalem and not the final distress of the last days. Other sufferings can be expected in the period after the destruction of the city.

Verses 21 and 22 seem to be a simple repetition of the same lesson given in verses 5 and 6. The difference is that here the disciples are warned not to be delayed or turned from their flight by false prophets and messiahs.

Verse 23, "I have told you all these things beforehand," is the answer to the question first posed by the disciples as to the time "all these things" would happen (v. 4). Jesus has basically told them the following: (1) Do not expect wars and earthquakes and persecution to signal the final coming of Christ. Persevere nonetheless; (2) *do* leave Jerusalem when you see the desolating sacrilege stand where it ought not to be.

Now we are ready for a wholly new section of the discourse, describing what the real coming of the Son of Man will be like.

51

"I Say to All: Watch"

13:24-37

[24]"But in those days, after that tribulation, the sun will be darkened, and the moon will not give its light, [25]and the stars will be falling from heaven, and the powers in the heavens will be shaken. [26]And then they will see the Son of man coming in clouds with great power and glory. [27]And then he will send out the angels, and gather his elect from the four winds, from the ends of the earth to the ends of heaven.

[28]"From the fig tree learn its lesson: as soon as its branch becomes tender and puts forth its leaves, you know that summer is near. [29]So also, when you see these things taking place, you know that he is near, at the very gates. [30]Truly, I say to you, this generation will not pass away before all these things take place. [31]Heaven and earth will pass away, but my words will not pass away.

[32]"But of that day or that hour no one knows, not even the angels in heaven, nor the Son, but only the Father. [33]Take heed, watch; for you do not know when the time will come. [34]It is like a man going on a journey, when he leaves home and puts his servants in charge, each with his work, and commands the doorkeeper to be on the watch. [35]Watch therefore—for you do not know when the master of the house will come, in the evening, or at midnight, or at cockcrow, or in the morning—[36]lest he come suddenly and find you asleep. [37]And what I say to you I say to all: Watch."

THE "BUT . . ." WITH which this section begins signals an important new topic: the glorious coming of the Son of Man. This is the real hope of the disciples, in contrast to the false hopes Jesus has warned against up to this point. This coming will happen only after—not before or during—the tribulation described in verses 5-23. "In those days" is a common biblical expression for the "final time," but it offers no precision as to when the events will occur.

In his description of falling stars and the darkening of the sun and moon, Jesus is using language frequently employed in the Old Testament prophets to dramatize the cosmic significance of historical events—the fall of Babylon (Is 13:10) or of Edom (Is 34:4), a plague of locusts (Jl 2:10), or the death of Pharaoh (Ez 32:7). Even where used in a general way, it refers to some historical event by which God enters into judgment with his people (Am 8:9) or the nations (Jl 3:15). It does not necessarily imply a dissolution of the cosmos. The point is that instead of being associated with the fall of Jerusalem, which Mark's readers would logically expect to signal the end and the second coming, these cosmic metaphors are applied to the time *after* its destruction, and hence they are not associated with any specific historical event. This text, then, further frustrates any attempt to predict the exact time or earthly occurrence which will herald the coming of the Son of Man.

That coming is also described in Old Testament terms, specifically Daniel 7, except that the Son of Man does not come *to* the throne of God but he comes *to do what God does*—to gather the scattered people of God (Dt 30:3-4; Ps 50:3-5; Is 43:6; 66:8). For this purpose he sends out the angels. The Old Testament hope was that the Lord would gather all the tribes of Israel to the temple in Jerusalem. Jesus radically reinterprets this theme. The temple is no longer the center for this assembly. It is destroyed, as he foretold. Instead the Son of Man will gather the people to himself. This can refer, of course, to the final moment of human history. But it can also be interpreted as the period of the church, the gathering of the new community of God's elect around Jesus, dislocated once and for all from the temple. Jesus, humiliated and sent to the cross by the temple authorities, now comes as the glorious Son of Man to replace the temple as the assembling place for God's elect.

The lesson of the fig tree now becomes clear. The disciples have asked *when* the destruction of the temple is to happen (v. 4). Jesus replies that just as the budding fig tree heralds the summer, so "these things" will mean "he is near, even at the gates." Verse 29 seems to be an echo of the "desolating sacrilege" prophecy of verse 14, the only other place where Jesus refers to a specific coming event as a signal for the elect. The Revised Standard Version translation, "he is near," can also be rendered "it is near," and even if rendered "he" it is not clear whether this is the enemy or the Son of Man. "This generation" will witness all these events—the fall of Jerusalem and the shifting of God's center from the temple to the Son of Man. Verse 30 does not mean Jesus predicted the end of time and the parousia within the lifetime of his listeners. The prophecy applies to the destruction of Jerusalem and its consequences for the new people of God. God's word outlasts all creation (Is 40:6-8; 51:6; Ps 102:25-27); so, too, does the word of Jesus.

While there will be a sign that the destruction of Jerusalem is at hand (vv. 14, 29-30), there will be no way of knowing the moment of the glorious coming of the Son of Man (v. 32). This is the Father's secret, not given even to the Son to reveal (see Acts 1:6-7).

The whole discourse ends with an important instruction for all Jesus' disciples: "Take heed, watch." The Christian, not knowing the hour of his master's return, must persevere in faithfulness to the Lord and to the Lord's work, given to his trust (v. 34). Mark lists the four watches of the night according to Roman reckoning rather than the three used in Jewish reckoning.

Finally, though the question was asked by four of the original disciples, Jesus' answer is meant not only for them but for all the disciples and (in Mark's view surely) for the community in Rome. We may take it too as extending to us: "What I say to you I say to all: Watch!"

52

Broken Is Beautiful

14:1-9

14 It was now two days before the Passover and the feast of Unleavened Bread. And the chief priests and the scribes were seeking how to arrest him by stealth, and kill him; ²for they said, "Not during the feast, lest there be a tumult of the people."

³And while he was at Bethany in the house of Simon the leper, as he sat at table, a woman came with an

alabaster jar of ointment of pure nard, very costly, and she broke the jar and poured it over his head. ⁴But there were some who said to themselves indignantly, "Why was the ointment thus wasted? ⁵For this ointment might havᶜ been sold for more than three hundred denarii, and given to the poor." And they reproached her. ⁶But Jesus said, "Let her alone; why do you trouble her? She has done a beautiful thing to me. ⁷For you always have the poor with you, and whenever you will, you can do good to them; but you will not always have me. ⁸She has done what she could; she has anointed my body beforehand for burying. ⁹And truly, I say to you, wherever the gospel is preached in the whole world, what she has done will be told in memory of her."

AT THIS POINT Mark brings us to the climax of his gospel, Jesus' passion and victory over death. The evangelist began preparing us for this already in 3:6 with the plot of the Pharisees and Herodians to destroy Jesus. But from 8:31 on, with Jesus' repeated predictions, the gospel really becomes a journey to Jerusalem and the cross. With chapter 14 the passion story begins.

Passover and the feast of the Unleavened Bread were originally separate feasts, the latter beginning immediately after the former and lasting for a week. In practice, though, the feasts merged into a week-long celebration called Passover, and "the first day of Unleavened Bread" could refer either to the day on which the Passover lambs were sacrificed (see 14:12) in preparation for the Passover meal that evening (14th day of the month of Nisan) or to the next day when the feast of Unleavened Bread officially began. Consequently it is not clear from Mark 14:1 whether "two days before" means Nisan 12 or 13. In any case, Mark's purpose is to show the urgency of the project to dispose of Jesus, since the presence of the crowds might set the stage for a riot if any part of the plot were publicly carried out on the feast. Rome was known for its repressive measures. An uprising hailing a new "king of.the Jews," however momentarily successful it might be in the confusion, could only lead to more bloodshed. The chief priests and the scribes, troubled by Jesus' presence in Jerusalem, seek to destroy him quickly.

Instead of immediately reporting how Judas' offer to betray Jesus played into their hands, Mark flashes a contrasting scene before his reader. Jesus is cared for at a home in Bethany, where a devoted woman pours nard over his head. Nard, an oil from a root native to India, was sealed in an alabaster jar to preserve its fragrance. A long neck could be broken to allow the oil to be poured. The word "pure" or "genuine" in the Greek is *pistikos*, which can also mean *faithful*. Is Mark playing on the word here, suggesting that the nard poured out is a sign of faith amid the surrounding faithlessness which faces Jesus? At any rate, the oil is costly, and the woman's action shows a magnanimous love.

Others present, perhaps some of the disciples themselves, are taken aback by her "wastefulness." The nard should be spent on the poor. Jesus' answer could be taken as contrasting himself with the poor, making this the only place in the gospel where he favors himself over the poor. It could also be a statement justifying the use of money for Christian worship, as opposed to a totally utilitarian approach. On the other hand, Jesus may be identifying himself, in a way that is still a mystery to his disciples, as the poorest of the poor, the suffering just man of Psalm 41 who cries out, "Blessed is he who considers the poor! The Lord delivers him in the day of trouble; . . . thou dost not give him up to the will of his enemies . . . even my bosom friend in whom I trusted, who ate of my bread, has lifted his head against me. But thou, O Lord, be gracious to me, and raise me up!" The woman is blessed because she is doing a beautiful thing for the man who is so poor he is already consigned to death. Unlike Judas, who is plotting to betray him, the woman is anointing the body of Jesus for burial. In so doing she is also consecrating his body for the resurrection. Though this is not explicitly stated in Mark, the "raising up of the poor man" is the theme of Psalm 41, which lies behind both this text and the betrayal passage.

Verse 9 clearly predicts a time of evangelization after the death of Jesus and before the second coming. "Gospel" here has obviously come to mean not just the news of God's coming kingdom (1:15) but the news of what has happened in the life of Jesus. In the Gospel of Luke, the "remembering" is done through the repetition of the Lord's Supper (Lk 22:19), which is the sharing of his body. Here the remembering is done through preaching about the anointing of his body. Both meals foretell a future event—the death on the cross and the final banquet of the kingdom. So too the preaching of the word and the celebration of the sacrament recall the past event of Jesus' passion.

The woman is the only model of the true disciple. She contrasts not only with Judas but with the other disciples who have resisted the message of the cross until now. They jealously guard their lives lest they lose them (8:34-35). She, like the poor widow, gives him what is most precious to her. In her generous gift of self she "signs" Jesus for his own gift of self. For Mark, and for his community called to martyrdom, this kind of discipleship is "beautiful." It is the good news!

53

Jesus' Passover Supper

14:10-26

¹⁰Then Judas Iscariot, who was one of the twelve, went to the chief priests in order to betray him to them. ¹¹And when they heard it they were glad, and promised to give him money. And he sought an opportunity to betray him.

¹²And on the first day of Unleavened Bread, when they sacrificed the passover lamb, his disciples said to

him, "Where will you have us go and prepare for you to eat the passover?" [13]And he sent two of his disciples, and said to them, "Go into the city, and a man carrying a jar of water will meet you; follow him, [14]and wherever he enters, say to the householder, 'The Teacher says, Where is my guest room, where I am to eat the passover with my disciples?' [15]And he will show you a large upper room furnished and ready; there prepare for us." [16]And the disciples set out and went to the city, and found it as he had told them; and they prepared the passover.

[17]And when it was evening he came with the twelve. [18]And as they were at table eating, Jesus said, "Truly, I say to you, one of you will betray me, one who is eating with me." [19]They began to be sorrowful, and to say to him one after another, "Is it I?" [20]He said to them, "It is one of the twelve, one who is dipping bread in the same dish with me. [21]For the Son of man goes as it is written of him, but woe to that man by whom the Son of man is betrayed! It would have been better for that man if he had not been born."

[22]And as they were eating, he took bread, and blessed, and broke it, and gave it to them, and said, "Take; this is my body." [23]And he took a cup, and when he had given thanks he gave it to them, and they all drank of it. [24]And he said to them, "This is my blood of the covenant, which is poured out for many. [25]Truly, I say to you, I shall not drink again of the fruit of the vine until that day when I drink it new in the kingdom of God."

[26]And when they had sung a hymn, they went out to the Mount of Olives.

IN STARK CONTRAST to the woman of the anointing, Judas, one of Jesus' intimate circle, moves to betray Jesus. The chief priests would welcome his collaboration since Judas could easily locate Jesus amid the estimated quarter of a million pilgrims jamming Jerusalem for the Passover. And he could do it when Jesus was away from the protection of the crowds.

In describing the preparation for the Passover meal, Mark intentionally recalls the feedings of the multitudes and ties all of Jesus' meals together with deep eucharistic meaning. Jesus' disciples ask him how to provide food, as they did in the first feeding story (6:37). They share here in preparing the meal as they helped distribute the food to the crowds (6:30-44; 8:1-10).

In Mark 2-3 Jesus' manner of eating and table fellowship were factors leading the Pharisees and Herodians to plot his death (see also 7:2). After the second feeding story, Jesus told his disciples to beware of the leaven of the Pharisees and of Herod (8:15)—that is, their desire for signs and wonders without conversion and faith and also the expectation of a miraculous ministry without suffering and death. "Unleavened bread" here in 14:12 sets the tone of Jesus' realism against this false "leaven." The lesson for the disciple is this: Discipleship means sharing Jesus' table, and sharing Jesus' table means sharing his passion and death with only the promise of glory beyond. That for Mark is eucharist and genuine discipleship.

As in 11:1-7 it is possible that Jesus' directions indicate foreknowledge and divine authority at a time when human powers are beginning to close in on him. On the other hand, if crowds have already swollen the city, and if there was danger for Jesus and his disciples, a signal could have been prearranged to conceal Jesus' location for the meal. A man carrying a water pitcher could be easily spotted, since normally only women did this.

Jesus comes to the Holy City to celebrate the night of Israel's redemption from Egypt (Ex 12), a night which Jewish tradition also held to be the night of Israel's future redemption. The meal is the setting for the betrayal and the eucharist.

In the midst of the celebration, Jesus shocks the Twelve by announcing solemnly that one of them will betray him. He does not mention Judas by name (as if the treachery is too horrible to do so!). But perhaps this omission is also intended to suggest God's role in permitting the tragedy. The passive form ("the Son of Man is betrayed," v. 21) is used often of God's action. The betrayal is foretold in Psalm 41:9: "Even my bosom friend in whom I trusted, who ate of my bread, has lifted his heel against me." The woe to the betrayer contrasts sharply with the blessing of the woman in 14:9. It also reminds the Christians in Mark's community how dreadful it is to betray one with whom they have shared eucharist.

Jesus uses the ritual of the Passover meal to introduce a new meaning. The breaking and sharing of the unleavened bread recalled the affliction of the people in Egypt. But Jesus identifies the bread as his body, his whole person, which will be present whenever the disciples celebrate this meal. However, the word over the bread is the briefest possible. More attention is given to the word over the cup (in the context of Passover, this is the third ceremonial cup, taken after the meal). Jesus gives thanks (*eucharistesas* in the Greek). Three Old Testament passages are evoked by his words: Exodus 24:6-8, the Old Testament sealing of the covenant by the blood of sacrifice; Jeremiah 31:31-33, the promise of the new covenant (though the word "new" is not used, Jesus' reinterpretation of the Old Testament symbol implies it); and Isaiah 53:12, "the many" for whom the Suffering Servant offers his own life, as already foretold by Mark 10:45. The Eucharist is therefore a sacrificial meal in which the whole meaning of Jesus' life and death is expressed. Since the cup also summarizes discipleship (10:38; 14:36), table fellowship with Jesus is also a commitment to martyrdom.

Some scholars think that Jesus fasted while the disciples ate the Passover meal. This would tend to highlight even more the fact that the central meaning of the meal is Jesus and his impending death. It is clear from verse 25, at least, that he vowed an abstinence from the fourth cup which celebrated the consummation of the covenant, God's coming to take his people into the fullness of covenant union. Jesus' abstinence here points the eucharistic meal beyond his sacrificial death to its glorious consummation in the kingdom, that day of the triumph of the Son of Man (13:24-27, 32). Hereafter the Eucharist will celebrate the death of the Lord until he comes (1 Cor 11:26). Eucharist is therefore a celebration both of the Lord's presence and his absence; it is both feast and fast.

Jesus concludes the meal with the second half of the traditional Hallel, Psalms 115-118, which should be read at this
point, noting those phrases which this moment highlights on
the lips of Jesus, such as, "I shall not die, but I shall live and
recount the deeds of the Lord" (Ps 118:17).

54

"The Hour Has Come"
14:27-42

[27]And Jesus said to them, "You will all fall away; for it
is written, 'I will strike the shepherd, and the sheep
will be scattered.' [28]But after I am raised up, I will go
before you to Galilee." [29]Peter said to him, "Even
though they all fall away, I will not." [30]And Jesus said
to him, "Truly, I say to you, this very night, before the
cock crows twice, you will deny me three times." [31]But
he said vehemently, "If I must die with you, I will not
deny you." And they all said the same.
    [32]And they went to a place which was called Gethse-
mane; and he said to his disciples, "Sit here, while I
pray." [33]And he took with him Peter and James and
John, and began to be greatly distressed and troubled.
[34]And he said to them, "My soul is very sorrowful,
even to death; remain here, and watch." [35]And going a
little farther, he fell on the ground and prayed that, if it
were possible, the hour might pass from him. [36]And he
said, "Abba, Father, all things are possible to thee; remove this cup from me; yet not what I will, but what
thou wilt." [37]And he came and found them sleeping,
and he said to Peter, "Simon, are you asleep? Could
you not watch one hour? [38]Watch and pray that you

may not enter into temptation; the spirit indeed is willing, but the flesh is weak." [39]And again he went away and prayed, saying the same words. [40]And again he came and found them sleeping, for their eyes were very heavy; and they did not know what to answer him. [41]And he came the third time, and said to them, "Are you still sleeping and taking your rest? It is enough; the hour has come; the Son of man is betrayed into the hands of sinners. [42]Rise, let us be going; see, my betrayer is at hand."

ON THEIR WAY to the Mount of Olives Jesus predicts the falling away of all his disciples, quoting Zechariah 13:7. There the Lord strikes the leader and the people are scattered, but only as a process of purification to end in the creation of a new covenant community. Jesus then adds a prophecy of his resurrection. As in 8:31, 9:31, and 10:34, Galilee is important in Mark's gospel as the place for the regathering of the disciples, over against Jerusalem, destined to destruction. Galilee was also the base of Jesus' initiatives to the Gentiles and thus symbolized better than Jerusalem Mark's community in Rome.

As in other predictions, Peter hears only the first half. He will not fall away! Jesus then foretells that before dawn Peter will have denied him three times. Peter responds with a vehemence ironically recorded by Mark again at 14:71 in his third denial of Jesus. Peter and the disciples will prove in this instance to be the unrooted seed that "falls away when tribulation or persecution arises" (4:17).

The group arrives at Gethsemane, a name meaning "oil press." Jesus selects Peter, James, and John, the men who had witnessed his power over death (5:35-43) and had been given a foretaste of his glory in the transfiguration (9:2-8). Mark, who has not been afraid to report Jesus' emotions in the course of the gospel, now describes the deepest anguish in vocabulary that recalls the Hallel Psalm 116:3: "The snares of death encompassed me . . . I suffered distress and anguish." Jesus is crushed under the impact of sorrow. He tells the disciples to watch, apparently not for his own consolation, for none of his previous experiences with them would give him any reason to expect understanding and sympathy from them ("sleeping for sorrow" appears in Luke, but Mark 14:40 attributes their sleep to drowsiness and ignorance). Rather it is for the disciples' sake that he tells them to stay awake for the hour of trial.

Jesus prays for life as any human being would pray for life and as the psalmist prayed, "O Lord, I beseech thee, save my life!" (Hallel Psalm 116:4). The difference is that he addresses God as "Abba"—the intimate, familiar form never used in Jewish worship. Its rough equivalent in English is "Papa" or "Daddy." This daring new name became a central acclamation in Christian worship under the power of the Holy Spirit (Gal 4:6; Rom 8:15). "This cup" is the equivalent of "the hour," but it evokes a rich Old Testament background as the cup of God's wrath (Is 51:17-23), which even at times the undeserving have to drink (Jer 49:12). It also evokes the reference Jesus has already made to the passion as his cup (10:38). There is likewise a reference, in the same Hallel psalm, to the "cup of salvation" (Ps 116:13), following a reference to the unreliability of men (the apostles?). After Jesus wrestles with the Father, he at length surrenders to the Father's will.

Though Jesus' prayer will be repeated twice, it is completed in its first version in Mark, and from verse 37 onward the focus is entirely on the disciples. Jesus addresses the sleeping Peter as Simon, his old pre-Christian name, evoking his human weakness. "Watch" in verse 38 is plural, thus being addressed to the group of disciples. "To watch" in Mark appears elsewhere only in the parable of the doorkeeper who is told to stay awake "lest he come suddenly and find you asleep" (13:33-37). There is a great lesson here for Mark's community. The chosen three were not alert at the hour of the Master's coming back to them, and they flee at the moment of crisis. The coming for which they were unprepared was not the coming of the Lord in glory but the coming of the suffering Jesus. It is for just such a "coming" that Mark fears his community may not be ready, the coming of Jesus in martyrdom.

Returning a third time, Jesus gently reproaches the disciples' failure to be alert. "It is enough" (RSV) may also be translated "it is settled"—that is, the question of whether the Father would remove the cup and the hour. No word of the Father is recorded, but the approach of the guards is his answer. "The hour has come." The Son of Man, final and victorious judge of the world, is delivered into the hands of sinners—by Judas (who again is not mentioned by name) and also by that God whom Jesus has addressed as "Abba." This is the mysterious paradox that is recalled but not resolved on the cross itself (Mk 15:34). In the Hallel, Jesus had prayed the words "Precious in the sight of the Lord is the death of his faithful" (Ps 116:15). But only his resurrection and final coming in glory will make sense of this handing over of the Son to the power of evil.

These are the last recorded words of Jesus to his disciples. After a brief show of defense on a purely human level (v. 47), they will quickly abandon him (v. 50), fulfilling Jesus' prediction (14:27) and leaving him to face death alone.

55

Jesus Is Arrested

14:43-52

⁴³And immediately, while he was still speaking, Judas came, one of the twelve, and with him a crowd with swords and clubs, from the chief priests and the scribes and the elders. ⁴⁴Now the betrayer had given them a sign, saying, "The one I shall kiss is the man; seize him and lead him away safely." ⁴⁵And when he came, he went up to him at once, and said, "Master!" And he kissed him. ⁴⁶And they laid hands on him and seized him. ⁴⁷But one of those who stood by drew his sword, and struck the slave of the high priest and cut off his

ear. [48]And Jesus said to them, "Have you come out as against a robber, with swords and clubs to capture me? [49]Day after day I was with you in the temple teaching, and you did not seize me. But let the scriptures be fulfilled." [50]And they all forsook him, and fled.

[51]And a young man followed him, with nothing but a linen cloth about his body; and they seized him, [52]but he left the linen cloth and ran away naked.

JESUS HAS NO sooner announced his betrayer than Judas appears. Mark could have described the searching crowd first and then focused on Judas. Instead, as he has left the betrayer unnamed up to this point, he now reveals him and names him as the leader in order to underline all the more poignantly the horror of this action by "one of the twelve." The arresting party need not have been large since Jesus was not armed. According to Mark, this group appears to have been given a warrant by the Sanhedrin itself, which had a wide authority in matters of public order where non-Roman citizens were concerned. However, the gospel of John indicates that Roman soldiers were also involved (Jn 18:3, 12). That Judas would have to identify Jesus for them indicates that Jesus was not well known to them, although the darkness further complicated the identification.

Once he has given Judas' name, Mark returns to his preferred anonymous title, "the betrayer" (v. 44). It was customary for disciples to greet their rabbi with a kiss. Here, of course, what was commonly the sign of respect and love is an act of betrayal.

There is a brief scuffle in which one of the disciples, who is obviously armed, cuts off the ear of the high priest's slave. This detail raises some interesting questions. Were all the disciples of Jesus in fact armed? Did they, as Luke suggests, pick up some swords in anticipation of trouble, because of something Jesus has said (Lk 22:35-38)? John identifies the disciple with the sword as Peter, and the high priest's servant as Malchus, a common name among the Syrians and Nabataeans.

The unsuccessful attempt at defense must indeed have been

feeble. There is no indication of anyone other than Jesus being arrested. All the disciples manage to get away. Meanwhile, Jesus underlines the irony of the situation. For at least two weeks prior to Passover (see 11:15-16) he had been available for arrest in the temple area. ("I was *with you*" indicates the posse was predominately Jewish.) His captors have had to resort to an informer and seclusion to take him. It is obvious from this that Jesus had a large following among the crowds and that any attempt to arrest him publicly would, as the authorities themselves knew, run the risk of a riot (14:1-2).

"But let the scriptures be fulfilled." To what scripture is Jesus referring? Possibly to Isaiah 53:12, "he . . . was numbered with the transgressors," or to Zechariah 13:7, "Strike the shepherd and the sheep will be scattered," which Jesus quoted at 14:27 and which will now be fulfilled as the disciples forsake him and flee.

To Mark alone we owe the curious detail about the young man who follows Jesus and escapes naked when the police attempt to seize him. We must distinguish two levels of understanding here, the historical and the symbolic. On the historical level, it has been suggested that this young man was Mark himself, the John Mark of Acts 12:12 whose home in Jerusalem was later an important meeting place for the Christian community. On the other hand, there is little doubt that this incident is also deeply symbolic for Mark. That he follows Jesus means that he is a disciple. That he is young suggests vigor, even perhaps faithfulness and wisdom, as in Daniel 1:4. The prophet Amos describes the day of the Lord's judgment as one on which "he who is stout of heart among the mighty shall flee away naked" (Am 2:16). If this is the symbolism, it means the hour of God's judgment has come. However, other texts of Mark himself may suggest an even more immediate symbolism. This disciple who continues to follow Jesus after the others flee is seized (14:51) just as Jesus was seized (14:44, 46). But he escapes by leaving the linen cloth behind. Jesus will likewise be wrapped in a linen cloth at his burial (the same word, 15:46) and will leave it behind in his resurrection, his escape from death. At the tomb there is a young man (again the same word, 16:5) sitting at the right hand and clothed in the white garment of victory. Thus the young man in the garden unwittingly reveals God's victory plan as the forces of death close in on Jesus.

56

Jesus Reveals His Identity
14:53-72

[53]And they led Jesus to the high priest; and all the chief priests and the elders and the scribes were assembled. [54]And Peter had followed him at a distance, right into the courtyard of the high priest; and he was sitting with the guards, and warming himself at the fire. [55]Now the chief priests and the whole council sought testimony against Jesus to put him to death; but they found none. [56]For many bore false witness against him, and their witness did not agree. [57]And some stood up and bore false witness against him, saying, [58]"We heard him say, 'I will destroy this temple that is made with hands, and in three days I will build another, not made with hands.'" [59]Yet not even so did their testimony agree. [60]And the high priest stood up in the midst, and asked Jesus, "Have you no answer to make? What is it that these men testify against you?" [61]But he was silent and made no answer. Again the high priest asked him, "Are you the Christ, the Son of the Blessed?" [62]And Jesus said, "I am; and you will see the Son of man sitting at the right hand of Power, and coming with the clouds of heaven." [63]And the high priest tore his mantle, and said, "Why do we still need witnesses? [64]You have heard his blasphemy. What is

your decision?" And they all condemned him as deserving death. [65]And some began to spit on him, and to
cover his face, and to strike him, saying to him, "Prophesy!" And the guards received him with blows.

[66]And as Peter was below in the courtyard, one of the
maids of the high priest came; [67]and seeing Peter
warming himself, she looked at him, and said, "You
also were with the Nazarene, Jesus." [68]But he denied it,
saying, "I neither know nor understand what you
mean." And he went out into the gateway. [69]And the
maid saw him, and began again to say to the bystanders, "This man is one of them." [70]But again he
denied it. And after a little while again the bystanders
said to Peter, "Certainly you are one of them; for you
are a Galilean." [71]But he began to invoke a curse on
himself and to swear, "I do not know this man of
whom you speak." [72]And immediately the cock crowed
a second time. And Peter remembered how Jesus had
said to him, "Before the cock crows twice, you will
deny me three times." And he broke down and wept.

JESUS IS LED to the home of the high priest Caiaphas where a
quorum of the Sanhedrin is gathered. There is no space here to
discuss Mark's account of the proceedings in the light of rabbinic prescriptions for a valid trial. We will simply follow the
text of Mark, which is also an interpretation of the events for
the Christian reader. Mark contrasts Jesus and Peter by introducing the courtyard scene at the beginning of the trial. The
servants of the high priest have been required to stay on duty
through the night because of the important proceedings in the
house. Peter joins them at the fire.

A capital sentence could not be handed down without the
concurring testimony of two witnesses. The authorities, antici-
pating the trial, had apparently rounded up all the witnesses
they could find, but their testimony did not agree. Finally, some
claimed to have heard Jesus say he would destroy and rebuild
the temple. Did the falsity of their witness come from the fact

that Jesus never made such a claim, or from the fact that they could not give a coherent version of a claim Jesus really made? The Christian reader knows Jesus foretold the destruction of the temple (13:1-2) and the building of a new community of which he would be the cornerstone (12:10). "Not built with hands" to the Christian reader means this new community. On the lips of the witnesses, however, it would mean a claim to divine or magical power to reconstruct in a moment what had taken years of human effort to build. To attempt to destroy the national sanctuary would have been a capital offense, but the evidence from the witnesses proves inconclusive.

The high priest then tries to get Jesus to clarify the conflicting testimony in the hopes that he will implicate himself by his own words. But Jesus keeps silence, forcing the high priest to put the direct question to Jesus, "Are you the Messiah, the Son of God ["the blessed"]?" In so doing he questions Jesus on the two titles Mark gave to Jesus at the opening of the gospel (1:1), titles which Jesus has avoided (1:24-25, 34) or accepted only with qualifications (8:29-30) until now. The reason for such guarding of the "messianic secret" was to provide time for Jesus to identify himself as the suffering Son of Man—a qualification quite necessary when he was enjoying great success in his ministry. Now, however, he stands before the high priest bound as a criminal, without power and about to pass through the ultimate humiliation of his passion and death. He accepts these titles now because his captive status provides this qualification needed to avoid misinterpretation. The messianic secret is out: Yes, I am the Messiah, the Son of God. And this same person you now see before you in chains you will see as the glorious Son of Man, seated at the right hand of God and coming with the clouds of heaven. Jesus is indeed King, the Messiah, the Son of David, and Son of God, but he will be fully revealed as such only at the parousia when he appears as the enthroned (Ps 110:1) and coming Son of Man (Dn 7:13-14).

It is this claim rather than the temple issue which elicits the high priest's charge of blasphemy. Why is this blasphemy? Is it that a human being claimed to be Son of God? Not in the refined theological sense in which Christians later came to understand the title. In the historical situation, it seems more likely that the high priest could accuse of blasphemy one who claimed to be the Messiah-Son-of-God on his own words, without having divine credentials. Under the circumstances these credentials would have been some divine intervention to save the Messiah from poverty, imprisonment, suffering, and death. It is the weakness and defenselessness of this man that disqualifies him as the Messiah in the eyes of the high priest and the court. The same accusations will be made by the bystanders on the cross (15:31-32).

The Sanhedrin judges Jesus as deserving of death, although only the Romans have the power of actual execution. Jesus is then spat upon and struck. He is mockingly asked to prophesy. Ironically, one of his prophecies is going to be fulfilled at this very moment—Peter's denial.

The scene is so graphic it needs little commentary. What a contrast with Jesus' confession before the court! Peter does what probably a number of Mark's community have done—denied their Lord. The denials build until, in the third, Peter invokes a curse. No object of the curse is mentioned, though Peter himself suffers its effects. Thus when Peter's weakness (see 8:38) is probed, he eventually becomes hostile to Jesus in order to save his own life. But the remembrance of Jesus' prophecy, triggered by the cockcrow, leads Peter to repentant tears. The "rock" has broken.

57

Jesus Faces Pilate
15:1-15

15 And as soon as it was morning the chief priests, with the elders and scribes, and the whole council held a consultation; and they bound Jesus and led him away and delivered him to Pilate. [2]And Pilate asked him, "Are you the King of the Jews?" And he answered him, "You have said so." [3]And the chief priests accused him of many things. [4]And Pilate again asked him, "Have you no answer to make? See how many charges they bring against you." [5]But Jesus made no further answer, so that Pilate wondered.

[6]Now at the feast he used to release for them one prisoner whom they asked. [7]And among the rebels in prison, who had committed murder in the insurrection, there was a man called Barabbas. [8]And the crowd came up and began to ask Pilate to do as he was wont to do for them. [9]And he answered them, "Do you want me to release for you the King of the Jews?" [10]For he perceived that it was out of envy that the chief priests had delivered him up. [11]But the chief priests stirred up the crowd to have him release for them Barabbas instead. [12]And Pilate again said to them, "Then what shall I do with the man whom you call the King of the Jews?" [13]And they cried out again, "Crucify him." [14]And Pilate said to them, "Why, what evil has he done?" But they shouted all the more, "Crucify him." [15]So Pilate, wishing to satisfy the crowd, released for them Barabbas; and having scourged Jesus, he delivered him to be crucified.

THE MORNING CONSULTATION may have been an official sanctioning of the night trial or a discussion concerning what formal accusation they would make when presenting Jesus to Pilate. Blasphemy would obviously be meaningless to the Roman procurator, so some other charge had to be found. Jesus had agreed to the title "Messiah," and its secular equivalent was "King of the Jews." From Mark's highly abbreviated account we can assume that the accusation was that Jesus claimed to be King of the Jews, with the political threat that such a title would present to procurator and emperor. The irony is that the Jewish authorities had found Jesus guilty of blasphemy for presuming to be a non-political messiah, and they accuse him before Pilate of being just that. Mark chooses his favorite word "deliver" to indicate the fatal destiny to which they consign Jesus by this act.

This is the first time in the gospel the title "King" is used of Jesus. Mark avoided it at the celebrational entry to Jerusalem (11:9-10) because even his Christian readers might have misunderstood Jesus' kingship as much as the disciples did. However, now that Jesus is clearly in the powerless posture decreed for him by the scriptures, Mark allows Jesus this title just as he did "Messiah" and "Son of God." He will be a suffering and crucified king. Hereafter most of the passion story depicts Jesus in his kingly role. To Pilate's question, "Are you the king of the Jews?" Jesus responds in an oblique way: "You have said so" or "The words are yours." Jesus has his own understanding of that kingship, and withholds the out-and-out admission which would allow Pilate to condemn him as a political menace. The chief priests bring further accusations, and Pilate urges Jesus to answer them. Pilate, like any judge, would have preferred at least some defense, but Jesus is silent, in fulfillment of Isaiah 53:7. Pilate's wonder takes on the nature of a religious awe or reverence, and we may surmise he suspects the deeply religious nature of the man before him and the hidden agenda on the part of the chief priests, which goes quite beyond their original accusation (see v. 10).

Pilate, now bemused by the accusation of political ambition in the helpless Galilean before him, hopes to use the practice of the festal release of a prisoner to free Jesus. The imprisoned insurrectionist, Barabbas, is already condemned. Jesus is not— but the crowd might easily be persuaded to ask for Jesus. Pilate, however, has not calculated what a select crowd this is, a wholly pro-Barabbas crowd, including perhaps even some of the supporters of the insurrection. Nor has he calculated how easily this crowd will be persuaded by the promptings of the priests.

At this point Pilate further miscalculates and abdicates his judicial responsibility. To determine Jesus' fate is still his responsibility, yet he turns to the crowd for a decision. If he anticipates a request for a light punishment, he is badly deceived. "Crucify him!" they shout back. A final attempt to save Jesus fails, and Pilate realizes that the fuse has been lit for a riot if he resists the crowd further. He releases Barabbas and orders Jesus to be scourged in preparation for crucifixion.

Mark is so matter-of-fact about the punishment inflicted on Jesus! The *flagellum* was a flogging chain of leather strips braided with bits of bone or lead. The number of lashes was not limited, and the bones or entrails of the victim might easily be exposed. The flogging alone could result in death. For Jesus, this is only the first stage of the torment that will climax on the cross. The "delivering up," as Jesus had foretold it, (9:31; 10:33; 14:18-21), is now complete. Judas delivered Jesus into the hands of the priests' crowd (14:41), the priests deliver Jesus to Pilate (15:1), and Pilate delivers Jesus to the cross (15:15).

58

Mocked and Crucified King

15:16-32

[16]And the soldiers led him away inside the palace (that is, the praetorium); and they called together the whole battalion. [17]And they clothed him in a purple cloak, and plaiting a crown of thorns they put it on him. [18]And they began to salute him, "Hail, King of the Jews!" [19]And they struck his head with a reed, and spat upon him, and they knelt down in homage to him. [20]And when they had mocked him, they stripped him of the purple cloak, and put his own clothes on him. And they led him out to crucify him.

[21]And they compelled a passer-by, Simon of Cyrene, who was coming in from the country, the father of

Alexander and Rufus, to carry his cross. [22]And they brought him to the place called Golgotha (which means the place of a skull) [23]And they offered him wine mingled with myrrh; but he did not take it. [24]And they crucified him, and divided his garments among them, casting lots for them, to decide what each should take. [25]And it was the third hour, when they crucified him. [26]And the inscription of the charge against him read, "The King of the Jews." [27]And with him they crucified two robbers, one on his right and one on his left. [29]And those who passed by derided him, wagging their heads, and saying, "Aha! You who would destroy the temple and build it in three days, [30]save yourself, and come down from the cross!" [31]So also the chief priests mocked him to one another with the scribes, saying, "He saved others; he cannot save himself. [32]Let the Christ, the King of Israel, come down now from the cross, that we may see and believe." Those who were crucified with him also reviled him.

HERE MOCKERY, NOT physical pain, is the most prominent element of the scourging. The troops who have accompanied Pilate to the feast to maintain order now gather for an entertainment break. They snatch a piece of purple material and throw it over Jesus, thus imitating the investiture of a vassal king. The crown of thorns was no doubt painful, but its primary purpose was to complete Jesus' mock regalia. With this and the other details of the humiliation, Mark is presenting a powerful commentary to his community. Jesus is king, yes, but only through humiliation and abuse.

The scene now turns to the way of the cross. In Roman crucifixions, the condemned usually was forced to carry the crosspiece to the place where the upright beam was already standing. Jesus' weakened condition leads the soldiers to seek help for him. Simon, a Jewish resident of Jerusalem originally from what is Libya today, is identified as the father of Alexander and Rufus, persons well-known to Mark's community.

In 1941, archaeologists discovered in the Kidron Valley a first-century burial cave used by Cyrenian Jews with an ossuary inscribed, "Alexander, son of Simon." Of course, it is not certain that it is the family known by Mark.

Simon is forced to carry the cross-beam. In doing so, he does what none of the disciples were there to do—carry the cross after Jesus—an essential trait of discipleship, according to Jesus' earlier teaching (8:34).

Just outside the city gates there was a skull-shaped rock formation called *Golgatha* in Aramaic and *Calvaria* in Latin. This spot is almost certainly to be identified with that rocky height now incorporated into the Church of the Holy Sepulchre in Jerusalem. Before nailing Jesus to the cross "they" (presumably the soldiers) offer him a narcotic to ease the pain. This, however, was not a Roman custom. It was a traditional ministry of respected women in Jerusalem to prepare a narcotic drink for condemned criminals to drink before execution. Thus it may have been prepared by the women mentioned at 15:40-41. Myrrh was known for its narcotic value. Jesus, however, refuses to take it. He wishes to maintain, in the face of the most intense pain, the fullest possible awareness.

Mark describes the crucifixion itself in the briefest way possible—three words in Greek. No need to describe the horror to his Roman audiences, who knew only too well what crucifixion meant. In 1968, Jewish archaeologists discovered in Jerusalem the first physical evidence of a crucifixion in antiquity. A young first-century Judean named Yehohanan had been crucified in the following fashion. Nails were driven through the forearms. A small diagonal crosspiece supported the buttocks, and the legs were turned so that a single nail (7 inches long) could be driven through both heel bones. The crucifixion of Jesus would have been similar if not identical.

The casting of lots for the victim's last possessions was ordinary enough, but it caught Mark's eye as a fulfillment of Psalm 22:18: "They divide my garments among them, and for my raiment they cast lots." The mention of "the third hour" (nine o'clock) is a problem here. It clashes with John 19:14, which says Pilate reached his verdict "about the sixth hour." Further, this verse returns to and duplicates the information of verse 24, and Matthew and Luke, who otherwise follow Mark's text carefully, are lacking this verse. It is also missing from the so-called Gospel of Peter, which otherwise follows Mark. There is good reason, then, for the conjecture that a later copyist inserted this hour, perhaps because he felt the need to fill out the practice of three-hour intervals followed in 15:33. On the other hand, Mark may, for catechetical purposes, have arranged the major events of the passion in three-hour intervals (from midnight on), and in this case, the verse could be a summary closure of what began around nine a.m. with the trial before Pilate.

Posting the crime for which the criminal was executed above the head of the crucified was well-known Roman practice. Jesus was sentenced by the Romans as a challenger to the authority of Rome and, precisely, on the matter of kingship over the Jews.

Since robbery was not a capital offense, the word the Revised Standard Version renders "robbers" should probably be understood as insurrectionists, like the zealots for whom the Jewish historian Josephus constantly uses this word. The mockery of the bystanders fulfills Psalm 22:6-7. Jesus was indeed crucified in his weakness (15:31; 2 Cor 13:4). He was sent to heal others, not to save himself from suffering. The leaven of those who wanted signs that would excuse faith (8:11-15) is now exposed in the sarcasm of those who gloat over their victory. He does not escape reviling even by the others crucified with him.

59

The Weakness of God Is Stronger than Men

15:33-47

[33]And when the sixth hour had come, there was darkness over the whole land until the ninth hour. [34]And at the ninth hour Jesus cried with a loud voice, "Eloi, Eloi, lama sabachthani?" which means, "My God, my God, why hast thou forsaken me?" [35]And some of the bystanders hearing it said, "Behold, he is calling Elijah." [36]And one ran and, filling a sponge full of vinegar, put it on a reed and gave it to him to drink, saying, "Wait, let us see whether Elijah will come to take him down." [37]And Jesus uttered a loud cry, and breathed his last. [38]And the curtain of the temple was torn in two, from top to bottom. [39]And when the centurion, who stood facing him, saw that he thus breathed his last, he said, "Truly this man was the Son of God!"

[40]There were also women looking on from afar, among whom were Mary Magdalene, and Mary the mother of James the younger and of Joses, and Salome, [41]who, when he was in Galilee, followed him, and ministered to him; and also many other women who came up with him to Jerusalem.

[42]And when evening had come, since it was the Day of Preparation, that is, the day before the sabbath, [43]Joseph of Arimathea, a respected member of the council, who was also himself looking for the kingdom of God, took courage and went to Pilate, and asked for the body of Jesus. [44]And Pilate wondered if he were already dead; and summoning the centurion, he asked him whether he was already dead. [45]And when he

learned from the centurion that he was dead, he granted the body to Joseph. ⁴⁶and he brought a linen shroud, and taking him down, wrapped him in the linen shroud, and laid him in a tomb which had been hewn out of the rock; and he rolled a stone against the door of the tomb. ⁴⁷Mary Magdalene and Mary the mother of Joses saw where he was laid.

WE NOW REACH the climax of Mark's gospel, the death of Jesus. The darkness that falls over the whole land from noon onward is a cosmic sign of the end of an era or a world (see commentary on 13:24). Amos prophesied, "On that day . . . I will make the sun go down at noon, and darken the earth in broad daylight. . . . I will make it like the mourning for an only son" (Am 8:9-10). Such darkness was also a sign of the death of a king (Ez 32:7) or the destruction of a city (Is 13:10; 34:4). In the original Passover, darkness falling over "the whole land" was the plague indicating God's wrath upon Egypt for not heeding the message of Moses (Ex 10:21-23). Judea has become Egypt!

At three o'clock Jesus utters the first words of Psalm 22. The Psalm is a lament of the just man that ends in an expression of confidence in God for the outcome. If Jesus not only evoked but said the entire psalm, Mark does not record it, presenting only the image of Jesus experiencing at death not the presence but the absence of God. If the martyrs in Mark's community are not experiencing the consoling vision of the Son of Man as the proto-martyr Stephen did (Luke's view of martyrdom in Acts 7:56), if they are mocked for not being rescued miraculously from death at the last moment, then they must know they are experiencing just what Jesus did. They may be delivered to the Romans by traitors within their own ranks and feel abandoned by God himself. The one consolation Mark offers is that they are in the company of him who was betrayed by man and abandoned by God.

Misconstruing the cry, some think Jesus is calling on the prophet Elijah to rescue him. The vinegar was offered as a gesture of refreshment for thirst, to keep Jesus alive a little longer, just to see if Elijah would come. It was also a fulfillment of Psalm 69:21, "For my thirst they gave me vinegar to drink." Jesus, however, utters a loud cry and dies. This is a cry of victory over all the powers of evil, a cry of consummation (which Jn 19:30 interprets with the words, "It is finished"). At once two important signs take place. The temple veil is ripped, signaling the end of the temple as God's place of revelation and worship. It is a forecast of the destruction of the temple brought about by the death of Jesus. In the last analysis, however, it is not Jesus who vindictively destroys the temple but the temple establishment itself who does so by executing Jesus.

Secondly, the centurion, representative of Gentile Rome, is the first in the gospel to make the Christian confession that Jesus is the Son of God. Not even Peter did that. What brings the centurion to confess the true identity of Jesus is not the cosmic signs he sees, but *how Jesus died*. It is Jesus' heroic endurance of death, not his miraculous escape from it, that proves the very issue for which he was condemned (14:61-64). Mark is telling his community of martyr-candidates that, like Jesus, they must be ready to go through death itself, and not run from it or expect a miraculous deliverance. Jesus, though a powerful healer and savior, is crucified in his weakness (2 Cor 13:4), and *that* is what wins the ultimate victory and the confession of the Gentile world.

Everything is reversed in this mighty act of God's "weakness." The primary witnesses of the saving events of Jesus' death, burial, and resurrection are not the Twelve, nor even the three chosen men, but a handful of faithful women (15:40-41, 47; 16:1). Roman practice was to leave the crucified on the gibbet even after death, at the mercy of wild animals and birds of prey, unless their families requested the privilege of burying them. This was usually denied in the case of those condemned for high treason. For this reason, Joseph's action is doubly remarkable. He is not a relative, and he intercedes for one condemned for treason. Already at Jesus' death the community which will be the new people of God replacing the temple is assembling: the Gentile centurion and the Jew, Joseph of Arimathea.

It was not unknown for crucified persons to survive on the cross two or three days. That is why Pilate ascertains Jesus' death from the centurion before releasing the body. Joseph, probably with help from others, perhaps servants, takes the body down, washes it, and wraps it in linen cloth. What is implied in the description of the tomb corresponds exactly to what is known of first-century tombs in the vicinity of Golgotha. A stone quarry had provided spaces for burial sites. Some of the more elaborate ones had an antechamber, with the body itself placed within an inner chamber. Where a circular stone door was provided, it followed a groove that tilted toward the doorway, facilitating closure but rendering the task of reopening much more difficult.

Mark closes this section with the mention of the two women witnesses because it is important that they identify the tomb which will be the scene of the Easter morning discovery.

60

"He Is Not Here!"

16:1-8

16 And when the sabbath was past, Mary Magdalene, and Mary the mother of James, and Salome, bought spices, so that they might go and anoint him. [2]And very early on the first day of the week they went to the tomb when the sun had risen. [3]And they were saying to one another, "Who will roll away the stone for us from the door of the tomb?" [4]And looking up, they saw that the stone was rolled back; for it was very large. [5]And entering the tomb, they saw a young man sitting on the right side, dressed in a white robe; and they were amazed. [6]And he said to them, "Do not be amazed; you seek Jesus of Nazareth, who was crucified. He has risen, he is not here; see the place where they laid him. ⁷But go, tell his disciples and Peter that he is going before you to Galilee; there you will see him, as he told you." ⁸And they went out and fled from the tomb; for trembling and astonishment had come upon them; and they said nothing to any one, for they were afraid.

THREE WOMEN WHO witnessed the death of Jesus (15:40-41) come at an early hour with spices to anoint his body. Anointing counteracted the odors of decomposition and manifested love and care for the deceased. The women obviously do not anticipate a resurrection. The things Jesus said in that regard have been forgotten in grief, as well as the fact that Jesus himself had already accepted a woman's anointing at Bethany as his burial-preparation (14:3-9).

The women have not asked any men to come along to roll back the heavy stone. Had they forgotten this elementary logic in their grief, or were they hoping to ask some passerby for his services? Mark does not say. Their first surprise is to find the stone rolled back. Upon entering the tomb they see a young man "sitting on the right side, dressed in a white robe." This is not Jesus but a messenger of revelation. Nevertheless, his very character, position, and dress symbolize and interpret the mystery of the empty tomb and the events which preceded it. At the moment Jesus was seized by the powers of death, a young man wrapped in linen was seized and escaped naked, leaving the linen cloth behind (14:51-52). At his burial Jesus was wrapped in a linen cloth. By his resurrection he has escaped the linen binding of death to sit at the right hand of the Power (14:62), dressed in the white garment of victory. The women are stunned with religious awe.

The young man (an angel?) explains that the one they are seeking, Jesus, is risen. The resurrection, revealed by the message, explains the historical phenomenon of the empty tomb. The messenger then commissions the women to be the first witnesses of the event—to tell the disciples what has happened and to direct them to Galilee. Here again God has set human expectations upside down. Jewish tradition did not admit women as valid witnesses, but here they are the first bearers of the Easter good news. They become apostles ("ones sent") to the apostles. They share in the communication of the angelic message to the community, just as they will share the ministry of prophecy (Acts 2:17-18; 21:9; 1 Cor 11:5).

Some contemporary authors say that Mark paints such a dishonorable picture of Peter and the disciples throughout his gospel that he means to say they have been rejected. Such a thesis fails to account for verse 7, "Go tell his disciples and Peter," which implies Jesus' forgiveness of Peter's denials. Furthermore, the promise that they will all see Jesus in Galilee is the fulfillment of the prophecy of which the failure of the disciples was only a part (14:27-28).

For Mark, Galilee, the place known for its mixture of Jews and Gentiles, has replaced Jerusalem. Galilee represents the new order of things and the new community where Jew and Gentile are equally disciples.

Mark's gospel promises a post-resurrection vision of Jesus without actually providing one. Perhaps his omission is in keeping with Mark's "dark night" theology of Christian martyrdom—that is, not holding out to the martyr candidate the expectation that he or she will see Jesus in glory before experiencing death.

In the concluding verse 8 the women fail to fulfill their mission, at least temporarily, although eventually their story becomes well enough known to be recorded in the gospel. The emphasis, however, is not as much on this failure as on the reason for it, contained in the last words of the gospel: "for they were afraid." This fear is not mere fear at finding an empty tomb. It is the religious stupefaction encountered throughout the gospel at the divine action taking place in Jesus (4:41; 5:15, 33, 36; 6:50) and the mouth-closing silence it evokes, as at the transfiguration (9:6) and the revelation at the cross (9:32).

Mark leaves the reader with the vivid picture of the crucified as the last living memory of Jesus. We have seen the empty tomb and await the sight of Jesus in Galilee. Mark's theology is tough. Signs will never replace the need for faith, and glimpses of the risen Lord will never replace the waiting of hope. Mark will not allow anything to replace the real experience of Jesus' absence, nor the longing for his glorious return.

61

Later Endings of the Gospel

IN ALL PROBABILITY Mark's gospel originally ended at verse 8. That is where important early Greek manuscripts end. The church historian Eusebius, writing in the fourth century, noted that accurate copies of Mark ended there. However, three important and diverse additional endings are found in some manuscripts, and, for the satisfaction of the reader's legitimate curiosity, a word must be said about each:

1. *The "Shorter-Ending."* In some later manuscripts the following addition is found: "But they reported briefly to Peter and those with him all that they had been told. And after this, Jesus himself sent out by means of them, from east to west, the sacred and imperishable proclamation of eternal salvation." This ending appears to have been composed by a scribe who, feeling that the gospel could not end on the note of the women's silence and fear, added a brief summary of what was known from the other gospels or oral tradition.

2. *The so-called "Freer Logion."* Known to Jerome, this ending was discovered in its Greek form in 1906 in Egypt in a fifth-century manuscript now preserved in the Freer Gallery of Art in Washington, D.C. It reads: "They offered this excuse: 'This lawless and faithless age is under Satan, who does not allow what is unclean and dominated by spirits to grasp the true power of God. Therefore,' they said to Christ, 'reveal your just

authority now.' Christ replied: 'The measure of the years of Satan's power has been fulfilled, but other terrible things are imminent. Yet it was for the sake of sinners that I was handed over to death, that they might return to the truth and sin no more, and inherit the spiritual and immortal glory of justification in heaven.'"

This ending seems to have originated in a Jewish Christian community which thought of the future in categories similar to those we find in Acts 3:19-21, where repentance is urged to prepare for the coming of the Messiah—what we would call "the second coming."

Neither of these endings has any ground for being from Mark's hand, and neither is held to be part of the canonical scriptures.

3. *The "Longer Ending"*. While not from Mark either, this ending appears in many ancient manuscripts and is considered as belonging to the canonical inspired scriptures. It appears as verses 9-20 in most of our Bibles. While added to complete the events from the discovery of the empty tomb to the commission of the disciples and the ascension, it does not follow the expectations of the Markan text, since there is no mention of the promised appearance in Galilee (v. 7).

There are, however, important teachings contained in this section. The ordinary disciples should not expect a vision of the risen Lord. The witness of the first disciples suffices (v. 14). The risen Lord commissioned the disciples to evangelize the whole world (v. 15). Faith and baptism are necessary for salvation, at least for those who have authentically heard the good news authentically preached (v. 16). Charismatic signs will accompany not only the preachers but all those who profess their faith in the gospel of Jesus Christ. This is normal Christianity (vv. 17-18). In addition to the powers of deliverance from demons, the gift of tongues, and healing, two unusual protections from harm are promised—from serpents and poison. Some Christian sects have interpreted the latter quite literally as an invitation to prove the truth of the gospel, with disastrous effects. But this is an interpretation that goes beyond the text, which does not command or encourage such initiatives. It is a promise, figurative and real, of God's protection against danger (as Paul was protected in Acts 28:1-6), but to choose such experiences on one's own would be tempting God, as Satan invited Jesus to tempt God (Mt 4:5-7; Lk 4:10-12).

The charismatic signs not only accompany the message; they *confirm* it by showing the power of God's word to change lives and to refashion history. Paul speaks of the same kind of activity of the Spirit confirming his preaching of the message (1 Cor 1:4-7; 1 Thes 1:4-6) and faith-response to the gospel (Gal 3:2).

The longer ending does contain important teaching, and it is accepted as the inspired word of God. Yet, since it was a later addition, even though quite early, it is not considered when interpreting the mind of Mark in writing his gospel.

Epilogue

Gift in the Night

MARK'S GOSPEL IS good news. But what kind of good news is it?

Early in the gospel we get the impression that it is the good news of *power*—God's power breaking into man's demon-ruled world to set captives free and begin the kingdom of God on earth. Mark entitles his gospel, "the Good News about Jesus, the Messiah and Son of God" (1:1). For a Jew, these titles could only mean that a long-awaited liberation was at hand—that God's justice would finally be done on earth, and the powers that oppressed his people over the centuries would be dethroned and banished.

Indeed, when Jesus makes his first appearance in the synagogue at Capernaum, he appears to be just such a "divine being," for unlike the scribes he teaches with *exousia*—that is, with authority and power. And this means not just a tone of certainty in his manner of teaching. It means rather that things begin to happen. A demon-possessed man is marvelously delivered of his bondage and returned to normalcy. Jesus heals and delivers, and this demonstration of power shows that he is indeed the stronger one foretold by the Baptist (1:7), the one who binds the strong man, Satan, and plunders his domain (3:23-27). And this shows that the kingdom of God announced by Jesus from his earliest preaching (1:15) has indeed begun in his ministry. Jesus' miracles are not small. He multiplies food to feed vast crowds (related twice in Mark, 6:35-44; 8:1-9), and he even raises the dead (5:35-43).

From the earliest hour it is also clear that Jesus intends to share this power with a community of disciples. He calls the first disciples even before he does a single miracle (1:16-20), and they are constantly at his side learning from him. Then he commissions them with this same *exousia* to deliver and to heal

(6:7-13), a power so great that it suggests the explanation that it derives from a man who has been raised from the dead (6:14-16).

It is clear, then, that the evangelist is discussing not only the past manifestation of power in Jesus' ministry but the present experience of that power in the ministry of Mark's community. Though not from the hand of Mark, the later conclusion of the gospel is faithful to this picture: "These signs will accompany those who believe: in my name they will cast out demons; they will speak in new tongues; they will pick up serpents, and if they drink any deadly thing, it will not hurt them; they will lay their hands on the sick, and they will recover" (16:17-18).

One would think that such a program would infallibly lead to success. It would be powerful enough not only to bring all Israel into the kingdom but also to bring the whole Roman world to its knees. But such was not the case. Jesus was crucified, and his disciples in Rome were thrown to the lions. How is this tragic reversal, this scandal, this "failure" explained? And is there still hope? What does Mark's community of martyrs in Rome have the right to expect?

Mark wrote his gospel basically to deal with that question: not the diminishment of power—for the miracles continued to be there—but the *failure* of power to convert the world and bring about the kingdom, with the even more shocking paradox that the ministry of mercy should end in the martyrdom of the ministers of mercy. Mark does the service of bringing his community the good news that lies beyond failure and martyrdom. It is Mark's version of what Paul has described as power made perfect in weakness.

As Mark relates his story of Jesus, he gradually introduces the reader to this mystery. In his brief description of the temptation, Mark notes that Jesus was with the "wild beasts" (1:13), perhaps a subtle hint that the disciples should not be surprised, when they face the great trial, to find themselves confronted with wild beasts too. Jesus tells his questioners that the disciples cannot fast as long as the bridegroom is with them, but then he adds that the bridegroom will be taken away one day—an allusion to Jesus' death (2:20). Jesus heals on the sabbath, and the ensuing dispute with the Pharisees leads to their plotting with the Herodians to destroy him (3:6). Despite his miraculous powers, Jesus is rejected in his hometown (6:1-6). John the Baptist's passion is narrated in considerable detail because it parallels and anticipates that of Jesus (6:14-29; 9:12-13). The disciples in the gospel, however, remain caught up in a theology of power and signs. Jesus accuses them of the same kind of blindness that has befallen the Pharisees and Herod—they want bigger and better signs (8:11-21).

There is a partial healing of their blindness when Peter identifies Jesus as the Messiah (8:28-30), but as soon as Jesus introduces his first prediction of his suffering and death, Peter resists, thus fulfilling Satan's role in trying to block Jesus from the cross (8:31-33). Let Mark's community of martyr-candidates hear! For Jesus adds to *all* (and not just to the original disciples): "If anyone would come after me, let him deny himself and take up his cross and follow me. For whoever would save his life will lose it; and whoever loses his life for my sake and the gospel's will save it" (8:34-35). To be a disciple it is not enough to keep the comandments, to love God and neighbor. One must make a clear decision to follow Jesus (10:21), and that means not only leaving one's past and present behind, but accepting where Jesus is going—to the cross!

Three times Jesus predicts his passion, but his disciples neither understand nor accept it (8:31; 9:31; 10:32-34). In fact, their response is not only to reject the idea, as Peter did (8:31-33), but thereafter to avoid it. They ask which of them is the greatest (9:33-34), they request the first places in the kingdom (10:35-40), and they quarrel among themselves (10:41). Jesus not only calls them to the humility of a child (9:35-36) and to peace among themselves (9:50), but in his admonitions he has that curious expression, "Every one will be salted with fire" (9:49). In the commentary I noted that this was an isolated saying of Jesus incorporated here because of the catchwords "salt" and "fire." But at a deeper level, Mark, through this saying of Jesus, was showing how petty such disputes were in a community in which every member is a victim readied for sacrifice, like Jesus himself. Furthermore, says Jesus, the aim of the disciple should be to serve and, like Jesus, to give his life for the many (10:45). Charismatic power is not for serving self but for serving others.

There can be no limits to this service. Jesus gave his life as a ransom. What this means for the disciple is illustrated by three women, one at the beginning of the gospel, the other two toward the end. The first woman is Peter's mother-in-law, who, in response to her healing, dedicates herself to serving the community of Jesus' disciples (1:29-31). The second woman is the widow who puts into the treasury all she has to live on (12:41-44). Jesus notes this act of total self-giving because it prepares us to understand his own. Finally, the woman who wastes the precious ointment on Jesus also knows what discipleship means—a magnificent waste of one's most precious possession. Whoever would save his life will lose it! Again, let the calculating disciples in Mark's community hear!

To them, finally, is contrasted the blind beggar Jesus heals at Jericho (10:46-52). He differs remarkably from the disciples whom Jesus practically has to drag with him to Jerusalem because of their fear and dismay (10:32-45). The blind Bartimaeus hails Jesus as the Messiah and, when given his sight, joyfully follows him up the road to Jerusalem.

There, in the holy city and upon the cross, climaxes Mark's version of the good news. Jesus tells the story of the Son cast from the vineyard and killed by the tenants, who then becomes the cornerstone of the new building God is erecting (12:1-12). Jerusalem will be destroyed, and the Son of Man will come in his glory (chapter 13), but in the present one can expect wars and famines and earthquakes and persecution—the end is not yet! (13:7-13, 33). The disciples are warned to keep awake in preparation for their Master's coming (13:32-37), but the coming for which they are not awake is the coming of Jesus in the garden of suffering (14:37, 40-41). This is where the eschatological trial—the temptation—takes place (14:38). Beware of missing Jesus when he comes in suffering!

The disciples' script does not call for a miraculous deliverance from martyrdom, for there was no such deliverance for Jesus. Jesus prayed for the cup to pass, but it did not

(14:32-42). He was betrayed to death by one who shared his table (14:10-21). Should the Roman Christians be surprised if they too are betrayed by one of their own?

On the way to Calvary, Simon of Cyrene was forced to carry the cross after Jesus. This Simon probably became a Christian, since his sons are well known to the Roman community (15:21). At this point in the passion, however, Simon probably represents for Mark the reluctant disciple who is constrained to carry the cross, unlike the one who willingly takes it up to follow Jesus (8:34-35).

At the place of crucifixion, Jesus refuses a narcotic that would ease the pain (15:23). He means to endure it all! There are no half-measures, no half-martyrdom.

On the cross he is taunted by those who believe in power as the only instrument of doing anything worthwhile. They invite him to save himself. He refuses to do so. Another important lesson for those in Mark's community who are scandalized by having to face martyrdom: Those who want Jesus to come down from the cross are his enemies! (15:29-32).

And so Jesus dies—crucified in his weakness, as Paul would say. Strangely, however, at the very moment of defeat there is a surprising victory. The Roman centurion, representative of the Gentiles, makes the first Christian confession, "Truly this was the Son of God!" (15:39). What wins his conversion is not a miraculous deliverance or cosmic signs but, by contrast, *the way Jesus died* (15:39). So too, Mark is saying, if the Gentile world is to be won to Jesus and the gospel, don't expect it to happen through God's miraculous intervention, nor by turning your powers of deliverance to your own benefit. Expect it rather by the way you die!

This would be a morbid romance with death, were it not for the fact that this fidelity is the ultimate demonstration of the power of the gospel and, in the final analysis, a romance with Jesus. And even should you experience not the closeness of God at that moment (cf. Lk 23:46) but his distance, even his abandoning you (15:34), know that it was no different for the one you hail as your Lord.

Mark's way of the cross is thus one of unrelieved darkness.

There is no ministering angel in the garden, no women who weep for Jesus on the way of the cross (as in Luke). Jesus shows no signs of power, such as make the soldiers fall back in John 18:6 or heal the attendant's ear in Luke 22:51. When offered a sedative, Jesus refuses. The only consolation he receives is the assistance of one who carries the cross after him—begrudgingly. The Christian should expect no better.

Might he at least expect to be sustained in his sufferings by a glimpse of the risen Lord, such as was granted to Stephen (Acts 7:55-56)? Or, failing that, might he at least lean on the witness of those who did see the risen Lord? Even here Mark relentlessly pursues his teaching on the "dark night." There is excitement, awe, and fear in the women on Easter morning. But it is not caused by seeing the risen Jesus. They see the stone rolled back and an empty tomb. What vision there is—of the young man dressed in white—only explains the absence of Jesus and promises vision later on. "He is risen, he is not here" is not a proclamation of presence but an explanation of absence. "You will see him" is, of course, a divine promise bearing divine certitude. But the seeing belongs to the stage of consummation, and the disciples will not see Jesus without another departure in faith.

Mark, then, is the theologian of the dark night. The Christian has enough in the example of Jesus and the grace of the Holy Spirit (13:11) to be faithful even to martyrdom. Glory is beyond, not before or during. That glory is wholly reserved for the day of the Son of Man, his coming on the clouds of heaven, the ultimate victory of God in time and history. This side of that, no glimpse should be demanded or expected.

In this respect Mark differs from the other three gospels. For Luke, the Holy Spirit in his powerful prophetic activity is the way the church experiences the continuing presence of the risen Lord. For Matthew, Jesus himself is the Emmanuel of the final times, God-with-us, the one who is present in the midst of the disciples wherever they gather and as they go about evangelizing the world till the end of time (Mt 1:23; 18:20; 28:20). For John, he who believes in Jesus already has eternal life; death is but a passage, for the believer really never dies (Jn

11:25-26). But Mark will not let go of the real and painful experience of the Lord as *absent*. No fleeting experience of the Lord's presence can satisfy the disciple whose whole life is now a fasting for the return of the bridegroom (2:20). The empty tomb is just that: a sign of the Lord's victory over death by going through it, and at the same time the perfect symbol of the emptiness the church feels without her Lord, for whose return she desperately longs. In such grieving and longing, how easily one might snatch at a hope offered by signs in the world that his coming is near! But Mark will have none of that either: No war or persecution or catastrophe gives any certitude. *The end is not yet!* Of that day and hour only the Father knows.

And thus there is no guarantee that the Lord will come in time to spare the disciple his own death, either. The Christian must be willing to walk by faith and not by sight (2 Cor 5:7) even to death. If the disciple has the power and the mission to heal the sick and to rout Satan, he does not cling to that power when his Lord takes the way to Calvary. Nor, arrived there, does he expect that power or any other to save him from the cross. Refusing short-term triumphs or self-serving schemes, the Christian, like Jesus, holds his only victory shout for his last breath (15:37). Only when he has given all has he gained all.

How can Mark dare to call this message *good* news? The parent who loses a night's sleep trying to quiet a crying child knows the secret: Love does not measure what it gives. And great love makes great sacrifice a joy. Because he loves, the disciple who wastes his life on Jesus knows that what he is doing is divinely beautiful (14:6). It is good news worth telling to the whole world (14:8).